S0-BII-534

BOUND
BY LOVE

BOUND BY LOVE

The Sweet Trap of Daughterhood

LUCY GILBERT and PAULA WEBSTER

Beacon Press   Boston

Copyright © 1982 by Lucy Gilbert and Paula Webster

Beacon Press books are published under the auspices
of the Unitarian Universalist Association,
25 Beacon Street, Boston, Massachusetts 02108

Published simultaneously in Canada by
Fitzhenry & Whiteside Limited, Toronto

All rights reserved
Printed in the United States of America

(hardcover) 9 8 7 6 5 4 3 2 1

Library of Congress Cataloging in Publication Data

Gilbert, Lucy
Bound by love.

1. Women—Social conditions. 2. Daughters—Social
conditions. 3. Family violence. 4. Sex role.
5. Sex discrimination against women. 6. Women's
rights. I. Webster, Paula. II. Title.
HQ1154.G49   305.4   81-65760
ISBN 0-8070-3250-6   AACR2

For Dale Bernstein and Carol Munter

CONTENTS

ACKNOWLEDGMENTS

We started to talk about violence against women in 1977 when Paula was gathering testimony from battered women on how they were dealt with in the court systems of New Jersey and Connecticut. This project was undertaken by the U.S. Commission on Civil Rights to evaluate community response to the needs of battered women. After a year of investigating concrete services and the lack of them, the project culminated in each state conducting open hearings on the obstacles to delivering adequate services to victims of violence. Each hearing documented how much need existed and how little help there was, but what was most striking was the way in which women who had been battered spoke about their struggle to survive and their inability to make sense of their experiences of violation at the hands of someone they loved.

The following year, Lucy began to work at the Jane Addams Center for Battered Women doing crisis intervention and counseling with women who had been or were being abused by husbands and lovers. During the two years she worked there, the stories the women told began to sound alarmingly similar. In spite of the brutal treatment, the threats of murder and mutilation and the resulting sense of worthlessness, most talked as if they were bound to these men in a final and irrevocable way.

Having already developed a common perspective in the context of the women's movement, we shared feminist assumptions about the oppression of women and the nature of power relations. We began to talk to each other about how violence against women might fit into our analysis of gender and culture. Although we were horrified by the reality of physical aggression vented on women's bodies, and overwhelmed by how widespread it turned out to be, we did what intellectuals do—tried to understand this violence and the responses to it as a phenomenon that was amenable to a reasoned interpretation.

We had an opportunity to formulate our first thoughts on

the subject for the conference in honor of Simone de Beauvoir that was calling for papers rethinking ideas presented in *The Second Sex* thirty years earlier. At the time, our focus was on why women don't leave the situations that violate and oppress them. We were dissatisfied with the answers that had been given up until then. As we read the literature and discussed our ideas with others in the anti-violence movement, we became convinced that the crucial variable underlying women's responses to victimization was the internalization of the cultural construct of femininity.

The paper was well received and generated a great deal of discussion. We were, however, criticized for looking at social relations in the family as the origin of the problems between men and women because, it was said, we had left out patriarchal social structures that gave men power and stripped women of it. When we were subsequently approached by Beacon Press to expand the ideas of the paper into a book, we felt it would be a way to address these criticisms and go further in our analysis by looking for commonalities in all the violations that are reserved for women: incest, rape, and battering. This book is a result of that process. To our surprise, as we worked on the violence data, we realized that what we wanted to say about women's responses to violation was the basis for a much more general theory of the psychology of women. We found that the cultural requirements for femininity ensure that all women will be vulnerable to victimization whether or not they are in fact violated by men. Thus the book represents what we believe to be the general case of women's responses to the world through the filter of acquired femininity.

We owe a great deal to the people who gave us support, encouragement, and information during the two and a half years we worked on the various phases of the book.

Without the women who so generously volunteered to tell us their stories of victimization and survival there would be no book. We thank these women for their help and are inspired by their courage and spirit.

Frances Goldin and Elise Goodman gave us invaluable suggestions on how to negotiate on our own behalf; Lenora DeSio gave us the gentle push and reassurance we needed to start writing a first draft; Batya Weinbaum called our attention to the importance of the daughter perspective in creating social theory; Flora Colao, Susan Schechter, and Katy Taylor generously shared their expertise and insights about victims/survivors and helped us to clarify our own ideas; Cornelia Brunner helped us get unstuck by offering a way to visually represent the contradictions of femininity, putting us on the right track again; Gerry Morse handled our manuscript with thoughtful respect, copyediting it in a way that was true to its intent; and Joanne Wyckoff, our editor, guided us through the process of creating a book with concern and commitment.

We want to thank the people who read and offered helpful comments on the manuscript in its many incarnations: Cornelia Brunner, Flora Colao, Peggy Crull, John D'Emilio, Beth Jaker, Jonathan Katz, Dianne Lasky, Linda Marks, Jonathan Miller, Joan Nestle, Suzanne Pred-Bass, Robert Roth, Susan Schechter, Katy Taylor, and Carole Vance.

For each of us, there were separate support networks we relied on during this process:

Lucy: I want to thank my family and friends for the support, encouragement, and help they gave me while I worked on this book.

I am grateful to my clients who speak of their experiences as daughters, and to my colleagues with whom I try to understand the internal and external forces that shape the psychological development of women.

My consciousness was radically altered in relation to violence against women when I worked at the Jane Addams Center for Battered Women. Although I was aware of the inequalities in our society and of the struggles between men and women, I was unprepared for the stories of gender war that battered women told me. I thank the clients of JAC for telling me about their lives and their attempts to cope with a painful, and as I discovered, widespread reality.

ACKNOWLEDGMENTS

For fascinating, humorous, and poignant discussions of daughterhood, I thank Batya Bauman, Elise Goodman, Vera Lightstone, Nell Merlino, and Susan Temkin.

Thanks to Peggy Crull, who encouraged me to develop my ideas about violence against women and gave me large doses of interest, enthusiasm, and support throughout; to Roberta Sklar, with whom I have had stimulating and rewarding discussions of femininity, violence, and everything else over the years, and for helping me to believe I could do this; to Lela Zaphiropoulos for always responding with warm, positive reassurance to my complaints about the process of writing a book, thereby encouraging me to give it my best shot.

Cornelia Brunner was a partner to me in my work on the book. She generously shared her remarkable intellect, considerable skill, tranquil spirit, and abundant patience by helping me to formulate theory, process data, edit, write, and not give up. I could not have done it without her.

Special thanks to my son, Jesse, who walks the tightrope of gender with ease and grace, and shows me daily that it is possible to be a whole person. He is my hope for the future.

Finally, I thank my collaborator and friend, Paula Webster, with whom I have shared the joys and struggles of co-authorship. Thanks to her unusual and wonderful way of looking at the world, we were able to enjoy the pleasures of intellectual work, self-discovery, and wild laughter as we attempted to comprehend, describe, and communicate our understanding of the contradictions of femininity. In spite of the difficulties of this process we managed to have fun *and* we are still speaking to each other!

Paula: From my friends and family I received what every writer needs: kitchen refuge, mountain retreat, stimulating conversation, distracting chitchat, and gifts of food, money, advice and intelligence. For these supplies, so generously offered, I would like to thank Emily Bass, Lane Bass, John D'Emilio, Margherita D'Onofrio, Laima Druskis, Deborah Edel, Jonathan Feldman, Ronald Garcia, Carol Kramer, Larry Krassnoff, Cinna Lomnitz,

Larissa Lomnitz, Lou McDonald, Joan Nestle, Connie Peretz, Suzanne Pred-Bass, Robert Roth, and Tajine. My mother, Helen Kinchelow, and her husband, Howard; my father, Woodrow Webster, and his wife, Susan; my sister, April; brothers Bruce and Damon, and my grandmother, Kate Lewis, have been a source of support and encouragement throughout.

Dianne Lasky, an old and cherished friend, lent me her skills as a writer in going over the last version of the book, helping me refine the rough spots with a gentle and loving hand; Linda Marks shared with me her unique sensibility and powerful intuitions when I was most in need of them—she made my telephone an instrument of salvation; I owe a special debt of gratitude to Abby Newton for seeing me through the daily struggles of anxiety and ambivalence with her solid sense of process and her genuine warmth and affection; Carole Vance, a daring and careful thinker, a wonderful friend, stood ready to read, discuss, and reflect on my ideas and intuitions or to meet me for a quick drink.

My heartfelt appreciation belongs to Jonathan Miller, who shared with me the most intimate moments of the creative process and lived to tell the tale. His original wit, generous spirit, soothing presence, and Zenlike detachment sustained and cheered me.

Finally, I throw a bouquet to my friend and co-author, Lucy Gilbert, whose insight, compassion, and fabulous sense of humor made the difficult process of collaboration an extraordinary intellectual and emotional experience.

For our final "finally," we would like to acknowledge and thank that amorphous and hard to define creature, The Women's Movement, which brought us together and provided the context for collaborative intellectual work in a community that continues to share our concerns.

Lucy Gilbert
Paula Webster
New York City
April 1982

PREFACE

I

There has never been a women's revolution.

Although individual women have resisted, rebelled, and refused to accept the violent acts against them, the majority of women endure and survive without challenging the status quo, dividing the world into good and bad men. Even in the face of overwhelming evidence, frightening statistics, and personal experience, women deny the implications of these demonstrations of male power and privilege. Instead, women accept their victimization with fatalism, believing there is nothing they can do to change men's natures and no way to wrest power from them.

As the latest wave of feminism washed over a generation of women, the world and women's place in it were revealed in startling new terms. We named our condition Oppression and ourselves Victims. The paradoxes of daily life, the dissatisfactions and dilemmas of choice were explained by our powerlessness in a male-dominated society. We spoke about the complexity and contradictions of being a woman given our situation of ascribed inferiority to men. In this public and private discourse, enough description of our situation was gathered to begin an analysis of our oppressed condition and to chart a direction for social action.

Though some women took up these challenges on a personal and a political level, the majority of women didn't experience this feminist analysis as relevant to their lives. Even violence against women, which engendered sympathy for *those* women who had been violated, didn't convince all women that current gender arrangements needed to be radically altered. Instead they distanced themselves from the violated women, feeling sorry for them, possibly outraged, but ultimately estranged from them. Women could not understand violence against women as an extreme but prototypical example of gender antagonism. It was easier to believe that the men who committed acts of violence were crazy, the women who permitted them to do so were masochistic or sexually provocative, or that they were the inevitable casualties of the unfortunate but predictable battle of the sexes. In short, most women could not claim this movement as their own.

What we didn't understand is that, on a cultural level, violence against women carries the weight of deeply held beliefs about the relations between the sexes and the oppression of women. Acts of violation on the bodies of women are emblematic of their powerless position in society. The woman's body, erotic symbol of men's pleasure and women's power, is made to surrender—not in passion and longing but in fear and terror. These acts of violation contain the essential beliefs about the social and sexual nature of masculinity and femininity. In both romance and transgression, women are defined as objects, either of love or hate, tenderness or cruelty. Although incest, rape, and battering supposedly deviate from heterosexual reciprocity—the norm of gender relations—they are in fact embedded in a culturally shared understanding about what men can do to women and what women must put up with from men. These acts merely demonstrate that men are prone to go too far and abuse their privileges and that women have no choice but to submit to their "natural" superiors, be he father, lover, husband or rapist.

Both women and men accept the culture's definition of who they are, which is contained in the gender stereotypes that prevail. Through the culture's mandate for the internalization of a gender package, he becomes masculine—powerful, authoritative, and active; she becomes feminine—powerless, deferential, and passive. Through gender socialization, the conditions for women's victimization are reproduced and assured. In becoming feminine, as we must, women are conditioned to act inferior and, at the same time, to hope we will be protected and honored in our submission and helplessness. Femininity, externally imposed and internally embraced, encourages the fantasy that our innocence will be respected and our endurance rewarded. Abandoning this fantasy means recognizing that our feminine qualities are a setup for abuse.

As feminist theoreticians, we believe that it is essential to change the focus of contemporary feminist inquiry from understanding how men become victimizers to how women become their victims. If we ask how women become victims, we must generate a description of daughterhood, since it was as daughters that we first experienced our oppression as women. We must ask where our femininity is created and how it comes to be used against us.

II

The forced march to femininity begins when we are daughters in the family. Daughterhood creates a common past for all women since it is the only shared structural feature of our lives. It is our first social identity and psychologically our most enduring one. We do not think that a woman's daughterhood ends when she becomes a wife or a mother. Despite differences of race, class, and culture, all women have been daughters. Even if we become mothers, marry or love men, we knew ourselves first as mommy's and daddy's girl, and despite the assumption of adult roles, we continue to behave and think and respond as daughters. Our consciousness and our feelings bear the indelible mark of our apprenticeship in the family, and in relation to others we act the Daughter. Given the cultural necessity to reproduce the two-gender system, the broad outline for our apprenticeship to femininity is basically the same.

If we can return to the site of our first experiences, the family, and recapture the feelings and thoughts of the daughter, we will be able to chart the internal geography of femininity and discover how our allegiance to gender rules was won and our potential for resistance diminished. If we can appreciate our common origins, we can gain immediate access to our oppression as women and begin to understand how all women are conditioned to expect less and endure more. It was as daughters that our psyches were fashioned in relation to the culture's representatives of the two-gender system, our parents. And it was the experience and the institution of daughterhood that prepared us to know ourselves as women and victims.

As daughters we first learned the meaning of women's subordination through demands for compliance and self-denial. Being a daughter means existing in a state of deprivation, since only selected aspects of the self are permitted to develop, primarily those which will suppress our energies and make us attractive to men. Our muteness, our passivity, our renunciation and sacrifice are encouraged in the name of love, first our parents' love and then the love of men. As potentially self-affirming behaviors are dropped from our repertoires, we lose energy. We are hungry. We live in scarcity. We learn that actively seeking in the world is not applauded for daughters, so we are not encouraged to call attention to ourselves, not to be too pushy, too forward or too demanding. We are familiar with deprivation since we didn't get enough support, attention or nurturance. Starved for nurturance, hungry for self-definition, we enter the world as feminine women, inexperienced with autonomy and fearful of its implications.

III

This book is an examination and analysis of the arduous and complex process that socializes women to accept victimization. Beginning at birth and continuing through adulthood, this process is intentional but not necessarily conscious, and it functions to reproduce the two-gender system in which men are powerful and women are powerless. We argue in Chapter 1 that the requirements of femininity and masculinity are culturally mandated and enforced across race, ethnic, and class lines in order to produce the uniform products of gender: women and men.

In Chapters 2, 3, and 4, we examine the daughter's relationship to her mother, the daughter's relationship to her father, and the dynamic triangle of the family romance, which highlights the scarcity of emotional resources in the family system and the competition for emotional supplies. In these chapters, we demonstrate that having learned to negotiate the contradictory demands placed upon her, when the daughter leaves the family she is already victimized by the necessity to repress her healthy sexual and aggressive strivings in order to behave in an acceptable feminine way.

In Chapters 5, 6, and 7, we show the ways in which the daughter's socialization to be a victim can be exploited both inside and outside the family. Chapter 5 shows the nuclear family as the site of potential danger when the daughter's trust is violated in incest and her femininity is precociously realized. This early violation confirms that being a female is synonymous with being a victim.

If she leaves the family without having been overtly violated, with the desire to lead an independent life, the daughter confronts the culture's rules for appropriate heterosexual conduct which ask her to provoke desire but to remain passive. Chapter 6 describes how daughters must wait to be pursued and chosen. Their hopes for romantic fulfillment are brutally crushed when heterosexuality takes the form of rape. A daughter who is raped becomes the cherished symbol of feminine martyrdom, a victim as she was meant to be.

Regardless of whether she has been an incest or rape victim, the daughter wishes to find a good man who will protect her. Through marriage, the daughter hopes to attain the rewards of the gender system, the status of wife and mother, and the possibility of fulfilling needs unmet in childhood. With a loyal mate, she can finally secure the love, sex, and acceptance she has been promised for being good (feminine). However, the man she loves is granted socially sanctioned power over her, and when she fails to meet his grandiose expectations to be nurtured, violence may erupt within the relationship. Chapter 7 asserts that battering is the predictable outcome of gender socialization where men are allowed to be victimizers and women are set up to be their victims.

Finally, Chapter 8 argues that it is in women's interest to challenge the gender system by recognizing that we must

emerge from the familiar role of victim. Having been conditioned to be victims in the family, this is no easy task for daughters since we experience "victim" as our true identity. Acting
on our own behalf in ways that violate gender norms may induce confusion and a frightening sense of being in the wrong
category (masculine) or of not being in any category at all. This
anxiety, experienced as a threat to the certainty of gender identification and normal femininity, is a major obstacle to the struggle for autonomy. The daughter in all women must renounce
her stance of self-denial and helplessness in order to feel more
in control of her life and enjoy it. In this final chapter, women
are encouraged to confront this anxiety and leave daughterhood
behind.

IV

Our approach in this book is psychological in method, political in intention, and social in scope. It grows from a feminist
perspective, in that we take the oppression of women as a given,
and it assumes that social change requires an understanding of
the internal as well as the external forces that reproduce women
as victims.

Our backgrounds in anthropology and psychology gave us a
dual perspective. Like anthropologists, we were curious about
the relations between idealized cultural values and social reality,
the rules of normative action and the arenas of taboo, the
meaning of the rituals which characterize relations of power and
relations between the genders. Thus we were interested in culture's manipulation of women as symbols of otherness, purity,
and martyrdom. Like anthropologists, we believe that a native's
view of cultural process, a woman's view of the culture of femininity, is the only way to know it.

Like psychologists, we began with the assumption that the
psychological consequences of the gender division are powerful,
become internalized, and are then experienced as a woman's
identity, her femininity. We were interested in the thoughts,
feelings, and behaviors of daughters, and used this information
as the basis of our analysis. In addition, we wanted to know if

daughters who had been victimized inside and outside the family were a special instance of the general case for all daughters or if they had a qualitatively different experience growing up as women. In books that focus on victims, these women are seen as a species unlike "normal" women. We suspected that this was not true, that women were not born feeling inferior but were socialized to feel that way. Yet this sense of inferiority, once created, influences every aspect of a woman's experience and her responses to all men and male violence.

Throughout the book, we speak of the Mother, the Father, and the Daughter. Abstracting from the variety of real people who fill these roles, we have created categories to illustrate the structural features of some family roles and relationships and the cultural rules which animate and guide them. We have tried to present an archetypal case, one that is compelling but not necessarily each woman's own. We hope to provoke in each reader personal recollections of her own story, using these categories as a stimulus to reinterpret experiences in the family. Of course there will be variations in content according to each woman's unique family circumstances, but we believe that the underlying structure will be the same. Gender constraints and gender prescriptions are not universal—they change historically and take different forms in every culture—but the two-gender system appears to be transcultural and transhistorical. In each case, masculine and feminine are dynamically opposed, complementary, and unequal.

In our interviews with women who experienced violence, we learned that they shared a common perspective of the experience of violation at the hands of men and that their responses had common themes. When they spoke of incest, rape, or battering, women all (1) blamed themselves, (2) denied the importance or magnitude of the event, (3) denied their anger and the wish to retaliate, (4) felt unable to set limits or fight back, and (5) found it difficult to indict the men who violated them, wanting to protect them instead. We concluded that this was an expression of the ideology of the oppressed and that women were alienated from their own suffering and rage.

Incest, rape, and battering do not make women warriors. Invaded, coerced, and physically threatened, women who are made into men's objects do not become man-haters. They only hate themselves for being victims. The battered woman says that she still loves her man and wants to work it out; the rape victim blames herself for not being careful enough, for not being suspicious enough; the incest victim claims that, strange as it may seem, she knows her father loved her. Few of these women are angry at the men who needed their bodies to assert their masculinity because they are used to being victims. They blame themselves for not being able to say no, feel ashamed of being victimized but cannot blame their victimizers, often denying the magnitude of the event and its painful consequences.

These responses struck a chord in us; we recognized them as our own and they were depressingly familiar. We knew that we had heard them all before, and felt them ourselves. We went on to interview women who had not had overt experiences with male violence and found that smaller, less dangerous, daily impositions on the wills of women were commonplace. We realized that these responses were feminine, characteristic of our gender group who is used to giving in and giving up. It became clear that gender socialization for women, the process of becoming feminine, is dangerous and debilitating, since it prepares us to accept victimization as our fate.

Bound by love to men, women face a terrible contradiction. We are dedicated to serving the group that benefits most from our subordination. In the family and in the world, men use their power to assert their masculinity and to defeat their opponents. When this privilege of power is acted out on women's bodies in acts of incest, rape, and battering, the conflict of interests between the genders is writ large. Made helpless and vulnerable by femininity, women are easy marks for acts of male aggression and rage; we have internalized the feminine stance in our relations to the world and to men, we both expect and accept our violation as inevitable.

We urge all women to read this book as daughters. Perhaps together we will begin to create the women's revolution that is so long overdue.

BOUND
BY LOVE

1
THE DANGERS
OF FEMININITY

One day, when Sara was barely nine years old, she sneaked into her brother's room and pulled a pair of jockey shorts and a white T-shirt out of his drawer. Clutching the underwear, she slipped into the bathroom to try them on.

Standing by the sink, she pulled her hair back with a rubber band, slicked it into place with water and stared into the mirror, trying to find a face to fit her new clothes. After forcing her eyes out of focus she thought she saw a more masculine face looking back at her. The effect was thrilling and disorienting, but just what she had desired. She looked like a boy.

Proud of her accomplishment, she went into the kitchen to show her mother the results of her experiment. Her mother, however, did not share her excitement and ordered her to remove her brother's underwear. Sara was not sure why her mother was so upset, but it was clear she had done something wrong. She returned to her room and made the undershirt into a bolero, a simple trick she had learned from her best friend. This time she went to get her mother's approval, sure she had remedied the situation, but Mom didn't seem to like it any better. She did not appreciate such imaginative play and was not going to encourage it. Her mother said that girls don't wear boys' underwear because they don't have what boys have, and she didn't see the joke. Sara felt defeated and humiliated. She learned that boys and girls must stay in their own clothes and in their own place.

Like Sara, many of us can remember the first time we experimented with the rules of masculinity or femininity by trying on clothes, attitudes, or behaviors marked "off limits." Usually someone told us that we couldn't change what nature had intended, that we had to remain girls or boys and find pleasure in the gender we were born to. These secret and transitory journeys into the territory of Otherness must have given us a glimpse of

1

what we wanted to know but we had to renounce them if we were to accomplish our primary social task, to replicate the social system as it is constructed. Breaking the rules for appropriate masculine or feminine behavior introduces us to the dangers of testing the power of cultural assumptions and fears of breaking unnamed taboos. Early in our lives we give up the desire to take such imaginative leaps over the boundaries of difference and lose our curiosity about being the Other. We become the men or women we were meant to be.

The division of humanity into the two gender groups, women and men, begins at the time we are born. Each infant is assigned to one or the other category on the basis of the shape and size of its genitals. Once this assignment is made we become what the culture believes each of us to be—feminine or masculine. Although many people think that men and women are the natural expression of a genetic blueprint, gender is a product of human thought and culture, a social construction that creates the "true nature" of all individuals. Human traits, capabilities, thoughts, and feelings are divided between the genders and come to be recognized and expressed in accordance with a complex set of rules and rituals that are learned to affirm this. Biological males and females are thus transformed by culture into men and women who are socially and psychologically conditioned to become masculine and feminine.

The division of infants into gender categories is based on the belief that men and women are different kinds of beings. The emphasis on difference results in boys and girls being raised and evaluated differently. Although each group is thought to be incomplete, it is assumed that they will come together as a heterosexual couple to achieve a fusion of the traits that keep them separate. Since the original separation of the two places them in opposition and the exclusivity of the assignment enforces their difference, only through heterosexual coupling can each come to appreciate the assumed benefits of complementarity.

The imposition of the culture's two-gender system creates an exclusive gender identity, one that feels natural despite the arduous path each child must follow to be recognized as appropriately feminine or masculine. Once imposed, this identity is internalized and experienced as an unalterable and inevitable reality. As children develop socially and psychologically the effects of difference are reinforced and rooted in the conscious and unconscious mind. The consequences of gender appear to be the result of an inborn personality structure and not the product of social conditioning and psychic structuring.

As men and women proceed through life, they are expected to "do" gender according to the culture's assumptions about proper gender relations. Men must be masculine to women's feminine. Separate and unequal, the two halves of humanity confront each other with expectations for difference, and they are rarely surprised. Conformity to the cultural rules is harnessed when children have no choice but to obey. The desire to have the right kind of child, masculine or feminine, is matched by the parents' need to reproduce the gender system as they know it, and the result is the ongoing re-creation of the present two-gender system.

The division of the world's infants into masculine or feminine would cause no dilemma if there were social parity between the genders, if differences were merely interesting but unimportant. However, in a patriarchal society the two-gender system mandates masculine and feminine beings who are unequal, giving one set social power and the other none. Relatively powerless, and considered inferior to men, all female infants enter a world that devalues and mystifies femininity. Society simultaneously denigrates and idealizes feminine characteristics, placing women on the pedestal and under the boot. The cultural system that defines femininity as inferior to masculinity and women as inferior to men creates a complex conflict of interests between the genders.

Boys and girls are raised with the cultural stereotypes for their gender as guides. To become what they are supposed to be, they must be discouraged from all behavior that does not conform to the notion of the basic nature of masculinity or femininity. Feminine traits must be stamped out of boys, masculine out of girls. To reproduce gender classifications and maintain the boundaries that divide boys from girls, each category must become what the other is not. Femininity and masculinity are conceived as opposites; therefore each child must be taught the limits of its human potential. The cultural rules of difference operate successfully when children can demonstrate that they know what they are and act appropriately masculine or feminine.

The model of masculinity that is presented to the little boy is based on an idealized vision of male power. Mothers want their sons to become the most valued type of male—the "Real Man." Although this ideal is not one to which all men actually conform, the concept dictates parents' attitudes for raising their sons, standards against which many men judge their own behavior and that of other men. Even adult men who reject substantial portions of the model, worry about how well they are "doing" masculinity.

The Real Man exhibits all the traits of a strong and self-assured person by being rational, competitive, proud, self-protective, physically powerful, and sexually active. Acting like a Real Man means standing up for your beliefs, pushing your opinions with determination and courage, even against seemingly insurmountable odds. Fighting for justice or doing evil, the Real Man approaches his tasks believing in the righteousness of his cause. If necessary the Real Man will protect those weaker than he, because it is his duty to use his strength for others. Even if he is tyrannical in exercising his power, he gains respect for the force of his will. He may not love conflict but enjoys a good fight since he can show his skills at winning—the only acceptable outcome to his struggles.

The struggles that demand a Real Man's strength are self-chosen. He asserts his individuality and independence even in the face of censure, and is often stimulated to bigger and better projects when he meets with adversity. He speaks with assurance and calm, explaining why tasks must be done his way. He never doubts the meaning of his life, is happy to be alive, and has much to accomplish. He is full of initiative and energy and undertakes all projects with full confidence that he will be successful. Sure of himself, he doesn't understand those who procrastinate because of indecision. He is a man of action, masterful and clever.

A Real Man learns his lessons quickly and applies his knowledge. Proud of his skills, he thinks it foolish to be excessively modest and doesn't consider it boastful to speak about his dreams, his plans, and his successes. He makes his way in the world by mapping strategies for what he wants. He knows he has to get ahead on his own and makes sure he is at the right place at the right time. He knows who can help him, is friendly to the right people, and thinks about the connections necessary to advancing his interests. He doesn't fear imposing himself by demanding too much of other people's time, resources, or energies. He likes to get his own way and uses people if he has to. If he doesn't succeed at first, he pauses briefly and sets off again to battle the elements. He never loses faith or confidence and just keeps fighting. The Real Man is not a quitter.

With his peers he is a loyal friend, but his friendships are based on shared activities—hanging out, doing or watching sports, drinking, camping, or arguing politics—rather than shared feelings. When he has trouble with his wife or his work or his mother, he does not expose his distress to other men lest he feel too vulnerable. Men are his competitors and he doesn't want them to have any advantage over him. He fears that an open expression of his feelings will raise questions about his masculinity. He prefers to stay cool with his buddies and thus ensure that his feelings are not misunderstood.

Although he can and must be serious, and bears the burden of power in society, he knows that a well-rounded person also has to have a good time. He likes to be outdoors, to be physically active, play, or at least watch, sports. His commitment to masculine pursuits is avowed and very strong. He likes men and spends time with them talking about masculine subjects, but not for too long. He has to get on with the business of life, and too much play is frivolous.

The world may think of a Real Man as rigid or tryannical, but this view does not threaten his masculinity. He has to be strong and sure about his objectives. Even if he blusters and rants and raves to get his way, he is forgiven such excesses because his authority speaks louder than his words, leaving even the most stubborn of his audience in awe at the passion of his desires.

A Real Man believes that life is a game in which there are winners and losers. The weak lose and the strong win. It is not a pretty reality, he will assure you, but that is the way society works. In this dog-eat-dog world, the goal is to get power and forget about approval. To win, it is necessary to get your hands dirty, to take risks, to sell out if need be, but never to suffer defeat, never to surrender. There is something feminine about surrender and passivity and a Real Man avoids them at all costs. Even when he can't avoid losing, he is respected if he gives it all he has. If he surrenders aggressively, with style, he still comes out a winner.

A Real Man likes women, but prefers the company of men, even though he shares his culture's terror of homosexuals, who are not "real" men. He lets women know that he finds them appealing but he is very choosy, interested only in the most attractive. He surveys a room, looking for his "type." He doesn't find most women interesting or intelligent, so he experiments in relationships with those who are at least pretty until he finds his ideal. He wants to be attractive to women so his dress conforms to the popular stereotypes of masculine attire. He can confidently be the casual professor, the immaculate businessman, the trendy hippy, or the macho outdoorsman, never believing that his real personality is obscured by his clothes. He isn't obsessed with his image, but he may spend a lot of time thinking about what he should wear in order to present one aspect or another of his masculine personality.

But women are necessary to validate his masculinity and heterosexuality. No Real Man can prove he is sufficiently masculine if he can't have sex with women. In our patriarchal culture celibate men are ridiculed and suspect. To demonstrate his masculinity a man must sexualize his simplest conversations with women. When having sexual relations with a woman, a man knows he is finally, without doubt, a man.

To succeed at masculinity a Real Man must always anticipate sexual adventure and be able to initiate and lead in seduction, smoothly encouraging women to surrender and entrust
what they say is most precious to them—their bodies and their
sexuality. An undeniably Real Man does not have to demand
access to women's sexuality; women offer themselves to him
with grateful sighs and great expectations.

If a young boy manages to achieve masculinity, as defined
and determined by the culture, he will find that the outcome of
being a man is to feel good about himself and his work, to feel
like a winner. In a male-dominated society like our own, in
which boys are valued over girls and men over women, boys will
grow up to believe they are more important, more valued, and
better than girls. If they can meet the demands of masculinity
they come to believe that they deserve the best.

The more masculine a man's behavior, the closer he is to
realizing the ideal. Yet exaggeration of masculine characteristics
can lead to persistent promotion of self-interest, cold-blooded
reason, lack of empathy, ruthless competition, and aggressive
sexuality. While these are considered negative traits, going too
far, taking masculinity too seriously, men are rarely criticized
for being too masculine. How could there be too much of a
good thing? Only when men abuse the power given to them by
virtue of their gender and become Dr. Strangelove or Jack the
Ripper does society turn a negative eye toward them. Men who
go too far, out of control, are destined to become victimizers,
using their privilege and their power for seemingly incompre-
hensible motives. Yet, masculinity, as determined by culture and
reproduced in the family, assures men that if they follow the
rules they will never become helpless victims. Hypermasculinity,
although not easy to live with, is never denigrated; it is rather
accorded awe and cringing respect. Boys who follow the gender
rules become winners and inherit the mantle of authority, legiti-
macy and power reserved for men.

While power is the reward for doing masculinity well, powerlessness is the reward for doing femininity well. A girl who
becomes the woman she is meant to be receives love, but never

power. The cultural stereotype for femininity may be as rigid and self-alienating as the one for masculinity, but its outcomes are different. The program for girls must make them into women, and women must be what men are not. Before they even learn the rules, girls are denied the possibility of ever becoming as special as boys.

The culture's message to girls about who they should be is contained in the stereotype for femininity. While masculinity is defined as a single consistent program for success, femininity is constructed as a formula for surrender. To be considered feminine a girl must suppress the positive traits that are labeled masculine. Each girl must reflect the mirror opposite of what is valued for men; she must learn to mute her strengths, her individuality, deny her own needs, and respond to the world in an emotional and noncompetitive manner. She must take every opportunity to demonstrate that she is a Real Woman, unselfish, flexible, cooperative, and altruistic. Her feminine behavior must conform to the cultural ideals for womanhood, the standard against which she will be judged as an appropriate member of her gender group.

When femininity is done well, girls become women whom men want to love, protect, cherish, and ultimately marry. Women who can stir the passions and imaginations of men should be ultrafeminine, magical child-women who can draw men to their place on the pedestal and make their requests for male help in a sweet and convincing voice.

Femininity creates the Princess/Daddy's Girl, the only woman considered exciting enough to deserve men's romantic attention. She should be fragile and not strong, helpless and insecure about her own worth, ineffectual and not masterful, confused and not rational, demanding but not competitive. She should feel like and act like a princess, waiting to be chosen and awakened by her master's touch. A woman who can pull off this version of the feminine ideal is promised the enduring respect of men and the unremitting jealousy of women. The stakes are high for the Princess, but to become the culture's sweetheart she must follow the rules.

The Princess looks to men for her definition and direction.

Since she depends on men to make her feel real she attracts their attention by flattering their masculinity. She assures them she is too fragile to stand on her own and cope with the harsh realities of everyday life. If her check book doesn't balance or the toilet backs up, she throws in the towel and waits for her boyfriend or husband to come home to set things in order. She is easily upset when things don't go her own way but isn't sure how she can take charge. Because she is fragile she expects others to do for her and make things just a little easier—easy enough for her to handle and not get dirty.

To get men to take care of her the Princess shows her help-lessness and inability to defend herself. With a roll of her eyes and a careless shrug of her shoulders she gasps in frustration, mocking herself for being a silly incompetent, while seeking a man who will tell her what to do. Afraid of appearing too self-sufficient or resourceful, and therefore unfeminine, she gives up easily and lets others have their own way, sulking all the while.

The Princess is also ineffectual. Although she tries to master the new technology at her office, she can't get it right and re-fuses to read the manual. When friends make luncheon dates with her, she regularly shows up late explaining that she left the oven on, or just had to finish the dishes before they piled too high. She is the Gracie Allen of the neighborhood and can't accomplish what she sets out to do. Bemused and confused, the Princess is unable to get it together and organize her life.

When confronted by the irritation she provokes, she lowers her head and whispers that she is sorry, or she is shocked—Who, me? She shows her fear of those in authority and her willingness to comply with their wishes. If her boss urges her to stay late to finish some work for his pet project, she finds it impossible to refuse but resents him for asking. She wants to please him, but more than that can't bear to have anyone angry at her. Masking her rage, she complies. She believes that politeness and acquiescence to men will ultimately protect her from their disfavor. She is unwilling to rock the boat. She becomes adept at indirection because making demands is unfeminine and therefore makes her uncomfortable.

She replays her delicate and rather demure behavior by dressing in styles that accentuate her softness and fragility. Hoping to attract the right man, she strikes a pose that is cold and unattainable yet approachable. Since she is not supposed to deliver what she obliquely promises by her sexy little-girl pose, she must be careful to present an understated sexuality, one that will not threaten her image. But the Princess is a little spunky, hedging her bets by acting innocent with just a touch of devil-may-care. Although she refuses to admit that she understands that men ultimately want sex from her, she is willing to flirt. In the end, however, her cleverness must not be taken too seriously. While she can tease and taunt, she must remain sexually aloof so men will not mistake her for a Bad Girl.

The Princess, the most desirable woman in patriarchal culture and fantasy, waits for a man to make her life meaningful. Although many try desperately to become the Princess, an arduous, if not impossible task, few are fully successful. It is difficult to stand around looking helpless when femininity requires so much work. Femininity is a schizophrenic condition since at the very same time that women have to act helpless and passive, we must also act helpful, enduring, nurturing, and assertive (but only in the interests of others). Like our mothers, we should be able to give until it hurts. In addition to confirming heterosexual femininity a woman must also become the tireless worker, the all-giving friend, the woman who takes care of others by putting herself last and making lives better for those more deserving than herself. So the Princess must take off her sequins and put on her apron to become the more ubiquitous version of a real woman, the Good Girl.

The Good Girl plays her role with a Saint in mind. She puts up with life's tragedies and stands steadfastly by when anyone needs her help. As a woman, she is not allowed control over the course of human events, but must be prepared to grit her teeth, endure her hardships, and go on. Her patience and good will in the face of adversity warm the hearts of all who hear of her sacrifice. She can take it and come back for more. Infinitely flexible, the Good Girl bears up under the weight of the world and her subordinate condition. She is strong for others yet her strength is worthy of praise only under adversity, when directed away from herself.

The Good Girl is not obsessed about her good looks or desirability the way the Princess is, at least in public. She is more refined, more sedate, and maddeningly practical. Though she isn't a prude, she refuses to wear clothes that are considered sexy. To her way of thinking, looking or acting seductive or sexual is morally distasteful and ultimately dangerous. Instead of looking fragile, she prefers to be "natural," to let her sense of practicality and good taste be reflected in sturdy and sensible attire. With her plain pumps, good haircut, moderate cleaning bill, and subtle makeup, she takes good care of herself but never looks too "fancy."

If her Gracie Allen sister can't get started because she doesn't know where to begin, the Good Girl is up at dawn planning good works. She likes herself best when she is doing for others, volunteering to watch your kids, make the coffee, and take work home, even before being asked. Tireless and self-effacing, she rejects praise for her work and considers modesty a virtue. Nothing is too much for her because she can handle it all.

While the Princess is reserved, emotionally withholding, the Good Girl experiences her life as an intense spectacle. She goes up and down, fluctuating between depression and boundless joy, feeling her way through the most difficult situations emotionally but never rationally. She fears being thought of as cold or calculating, even intellectual, and when she wants to get the best for herself and refuses to compromise, she feels she is being selfish —which doesn't sit right with her because that means she's acting like a man. So tirelessly she nurtures until she is ready to fall, which she does with a self-satisfied smile on her face. She makes others happy, thank God.

Instead of making her needs known, the Good Girl forgets to put herself in the picture, assertion coming with difficulty and seeming unfeminine. She plays the waiting game, looking for the right time, the precisely correct moment to state her feelings. She never gets angry when her desires are frustrated;

she is happy if you are happy. When conflicts arise she finds a way to play the mediator, to stress the futility of yelling or screaming or trying to get your way. She hates dissension and looks for the middle road, the common good. She is adept at compromise and accommodation, which she finesses with a tolerance that leaves others in her debt. She doesn't carp and complain about the silly things that occupy the more sensitive Princess, who is upset when things don't go her way. The Good Girl navigates through conflict and competition by denying her desire to win and burying her terror of losing. She withdraws when the action gets hot, claiming that the sidelines are fine for her.

The final model for femininity is the Bad Girl, the only woman who lives under the threat of excommunication from the feminine sorority because she doesn't follow the rules of self-denial and compliance. While the Good Girl timidly agrees to other people's desires, and the Princess sweetly demands what she wants, the Bad Girl calculates the costs and benefits of her actions, with a tough and unrelenting rationality. By daring to take herself seriously—like a man—she pursues her desires, even at the risk of appearing dangerous and unfeminine. She seeks pleasure and wants to control her own gratification. She strikes fear in the hearts of both men and women because she seems to be an anomaly of femininity, someone who misunderstands the limits of her gender.

A woman who refuses to act like the Princess or the Good Girl will surely be accused of being bad, the worst insult that can be directed at women, who are supposed to be good before all else. Being bad means not acting like a girl, crossing the line into masculinity, and threatening the assumed natural division between the sexes. No mother wants her daughter to be considered bad; no woman wants to live with that label as a permanent stigma. If a woman acts out of gender, trying on the masculine privileges, mannerisms, attitudes, or feelings that are off limits, society warns her that she will come to a bad end. A Bad Girl gets hurt, ends up in jail, suffers for her transgressions, and ultimately is alone. Had she only been good and acted like girls are supposed to, she would not find herself abandoned by the company of good women who can now feel better about their own sacrifices to femininity, or the real men whose excitement turns to boredom and then pity.

Little girls learn the complex structure of femininity as they grow up in the family and adopt it as a self-chosen identity after a time. They internalize the construct and take it on as a psychological identity, the only way to know the self—feeling secure when following the prescribed rules. Women come to act, think, and feel feminine, viewing the world and all social relations through the lens of the gender assignment. It feels natural to act like a woman and unnatural to deviate from that "authentic" identity. Acting unfeminine, or feeling out of gender, produces anxiety. A woman who is tempted to stand up for herself, act like a man by being competitive, self-directed, or selfish, experiences confusion about herself and worries that she is being bad, unfeminine, possibly a freak or an unnatural woman. This anxiety has to do with the fear of gender loss—the fear of being beyond the boundaries of femininity, without a solid identity. Without a secure sense of who she is, who she is supposed to be, a woman fears stepping out of the "natural" constraints. Understandably she wants to be normal.

Femininity, like masculinity, is enforced by external threats as well. A woman who tests the limits of gender by pushing beyond the definition of femininity is threatened with loss of approval, love, and male attention. By being pushy, aggressive, assertive, or selfish, she can lose her job, her boyfriend, or her mother's concern. Social conformity maintains the gender system, keeping women acting like women and men acting like men. The fears of rejection and loss of love, coupled with the internal threat of being out of control, going too far, not really acting like a woman, keep all women committed to a social and psychological identity that requires the suppression of autonomous and aggressive desires. Doing femininity well receives the praise of society and the rewards of being an acceptable heterosexual woman, one who can get her man and keep him. If she is good and adheres to the models that the culture values for women, she will come to be known and know herself as a Real Woman, ready to live her life as a subordinate to men without questioning the primary mechanism that reproduces her subordination—the acquisition of femininity.

Since girls cannot be boys, or act like them, girls must accept the script for femininity and live with the contradiction of acting both the fragile femme and the enduring Mother Courage, responding to life with the needs of a dependent child and the strength of an enduring martyr. If they can balance assertion that is not too assertive with dependency that is not too dependent, they are promised the respect of men, their love, and their benevolence. The applause for being good and the threats to self-esteem for being bad keep women in their place in the two-gender system. Women renounce what is self-fulfilling in order to become heterosexual successes.

Because women must "do" femininity in a patriarchal society in which men are more valued than women, being a woman means being subordinate. Boys get more power, more privilege, and, when they are adults, more of what society offers in terms of pleasure and control. Girls get less. They have to take what is offered and not ask for more. Eventually femininity is equated with inferiority and acceptance of deprivation. The conclusion that girls draw from observing and participating in a society that values masculine over feminine is that they must be less deserving, less special and important than boys. Repeated experience with deprivation encourages women to agree with the cultural definition that they are less and shouldn't ask for too much. Femininity, which requires women to be passive, quiet, selfless, and subordinate, sets women up to expect to be the losers and not the winners in the world. Conditioned to accept their own deprivation as "natural," women are poorly prepared to defend their own interests, ask for what they need, or fight for what they want.

Women who follow the rules for femininity come to feel like victims, helpless before the demands of other people, and unable to put their needs first. Refusing to let other people have their way feels bad—uncomfortable and threatening. Women who can't say no to the daily demands for their compliance end up feeling taken advantage of—used. But that seems preferable to feeling selfish. Women who say no, draw boundaries to protect what they think is important, court the danger of other people's anger, irritation, or displeasure. If they are not "good," they fear being "bad." But if they are "good girls," they often end up feeling used, abused, and victimized.

Women who are committed to being good, even when it serves others and not themselves, act out their feminine conditioning. Afraid to be thought rude, unable to draw the line that ensures their own comfort and gratification, they are helpless in situations where other people's needs for satisfaction seem to be more urgent than their own. Acting like the Good Girl even when it feels painful and self-defeating, is the only strategy that is familiar, the only one that feels acceptable and right. Women come to believe that they are less, deserve less, and shouldn't complain, confront, or struggle to get what they need.

So women complain about being take advantage of, but fail to understand why it feels so difficult to defend ourselves. Even in the simplest daily experiences we expect less and consequently get less. We watch ourselves giving up our place in line because we are afraid to protest; we submit to a bad haircut, unable to stop the scissors or walk out. Afraid of being thought too narcissistic, we suffer silently. Some of us spend more time than we want to with friends, children, lovers, and husbands, saying that the others' needs come first. We don't want to disappoint or cause any pain. Women stand ready to serve even when exhausted and indifferent. When someone strongly disagrees with our opinions we are mute, pondering the necessity of speaking up at all. Feeling powerless to assert ourselves, and terrified at the potency of our anger, we retreat into silence, speaking obliquely and indirectly about what we want.

We deny our anger when events don't turn out to our satisfaction and deny our disappointment when our desires are not fulfilled. We blame ourselves for the rejections, power trips, and cruelties of friends and lovers, saying we must have done something to deserve it. We find it hard to believe that people aren't as good as we would like them to be and assume responsibility for unpleasant situations in our lives, thinking we are in control when in fact we are not. If a woman doesn't get the job she wants she usually assumes she wasn't good enough, if she has a fight with her boyfriend she assumes it was her fault, that he was right and she was wrong. Never suspicious of other people's motives, never sure she can trust her feelings, women assume that everybody will protect their interests if they don't make trouble.

The program for femininity and the internal sense of security that keep women hooked on being what they are supposed to be leave them unprepared to define or defend their own interests. Ready to deny the dangers of surrendering to the will of others, women cheerfully walk into situations where defeat is inevitable. We come out feeling bad about ourselves, but never angry, never able to take the reins and get what we want.

Like a bottomless well, the truly feminine woman in all of us is a never-ending source of compassion and nurturance for others. She feels real when she is needed; she sees self-directed choice as something that will alienate her from those whom she cares most about—everybody but herself. Being good for others feels better than being good to herself. Women refuse to act like winners for fear of losing love, respect, or the good will of men and women who they think are better than they and more deserving of having their needs met. Wanting to be good, to be well thought of, to be liked, women passively endure impositions on their time, energy, and will in order to hold onto the good opinion of others. Fearing to ask for more or better, anxious about saying no and refusing to serve, the feminine woman walks a path that leads to self-denial and compliance—the only path for which her conditioning to femininity prepares her.

Because adhering to femininity seems natural, and because this "natural" condition strips women of the resources they need to stand up for themselves and fight back, most women believe that their victimization is inevitable. Since women are frightened of being called selfish, bad, or unfeminine, they often choose to be the losers instead of the winners. Winning assumes that one is better than someone else and doesn't fit in with the feminine self-image. A Real Woman says that it isn't important whether you win or lose, it's how you play the game. And she plays according to the rules of femininity, thereby ensuring her own defeat. Each time she loses, her femininity is validated; she is now the woman she was meant to be.

The woman who plays the Good Girl is promised some compensation for her efforts—the love of a man. The man, romanticised and overrated in the culture, will make up for the deprivations she suffers and assure the woman of her normalcy and worth. A man can lift the veil of social inferiority that women are forced to wear and elevate her above the generally denigrated category of Woman. With a man by her side she feels safer and more valuable, better able to deny her lack of social, economic and political power. Without a man she will be considered a heterosexual failure, a reject, a poor pitiable creature doomed to invisibility and celibacy. Her aloneness is the living proof of her inability to give, her failure to be feminine.

Masculinity and femininity are played out in the social relations between the sexes. Given the distribution of power and privilege, the relationship is always tinged with the residues of inequality; women must conspicuously demonstrate their admiration for the powerful and their willingness to serve; while men must express their respect for the powerless and their desire to protect. The contradictions of loving those who have more power than you are muted by the ideology of heterosexual romance, which assumes that women choose men because they experience an irresistible attraction to them. Yet a woman *must* choose a man if she is to fulfill her feminine destiny. Without a man she cannot be a "real woman," the only kind men are interested in.

To have their femininity validated, women must gain men's attention and approval. Women go about pleasing men with a single-minded energy they can rarely muster for themselves. Hungry for male recognition and fascinated by masculine power, women dedicate themselves to seeing that men get their way. Men's praise, even when grudgingly given, feels like a warm blanket of security. Putting men's interests first may seem to be a burden but the feminine woman smiles; nothing is too much for the man she loves. If she is successful in making him feel important, she can rest easy, knowing she has done her job well. She now feels worthy and finally visible.

But men demand a lot of women's services to make life warm and cozy. Sometimes a man forgets the limits of his social power and asks for too much, yet unreasonable demands on a woman's time, energy, and nurturing capacities are interpreted as his "needing" her, and above all else she wants to be needed. She understands and is grateful that someone of his stature wants so much from someone like her. She explains that men are tyrants but usually underneath they are babies. "Just another kid to take care of," she tells her friends. But in truth she loves him more because he can lean on her, is willing to put up with his "craziness" because he loves her.

And she forgives him because she knows that men go off sometimes, they are under pressure at work, they need to let off steam—men are like that. She is willing to become his emotional punching bag because he isn't really trying to hurt *her*, he just needs to let it out. She doesn't mind being a victim for a little while because women are like that. She keeps on keeping on. In this way she stops blaming him and relieves him of the responsibility to apologize. She says it was her fault, and she will try to stop complaining, acting so unfeminine, and be a better lover, wife, or girlfriend. She promises him and herself that she will be less angry in the future. The panic passes. He isn't leaving. She rededicates herself to being a good girl, hoping he will treat her better.

Femininity strips a woman of her desire to defend her own interests or to get what she wants from men. She is unprepared to act like a man with men. She says that she just couldn't disappoint him, will not ignore him, and can't change him. She makes jokes about the battle of the sexes with bitterness and resignation. Women have been conditioned, both socially and intrapsychically, to accept the ideology of gender relations and believe there is nothing they can do. Men must win. That's what makes them men. Women have no choice. They have to take what they can get and pretend it is enough.

THE DANGERS OF FEMININITY

Conditioned to be feminine, not masculine, women are set up to participate in their own deprivation, especially in their relations with men. Ambivalence about self-worth jockeys with fear of rejection, making a powerful social mandate to serve men feel like a compulsion, natural and even gratifying. Challenging men's authority feels dangerous. Disagreeing with their opinions is an act of insubordination creating a palpable anxiety. It is often easier to be good for him than to be "bad," risking his anger. If men are given power over women in culture and society, women can be thanked for promoting male interests. Even in the face of cruelty and cold indifference, women are junkies for male approval and do almost anything to have it delivered to the door.

Women's responses to impositions from men are predictable. Women endure the dissatisfactions of the gender system, sharing the culture's belief that men must never have their masculinity threatened. A woman who dares to challenge this system risks the anxiety of being out of gender—unnatural and therefore unappealing. She clenches her teeth and remains silent even when feeling violated by his demands. The sadness passes and the anger fades. If he is a "real" man, she as his victim is a "real" woman.

2
MOTHERS AND DAUGHTERS
The Creation of the Good Girl

Femininity, with its internal contradictions, is a complex construct. There are many different ways to be feminine. Depending on class, ethnic, family background, and other variables related to present historical conditions, daughters are exposed to and encouraged in different modes of femininity. The underlying structure of that femininity is the same, however, regardless of the particular selection, packaging, or emphasis. Femininity is always, at bottom, a formula for surrender. It is a way to accept second place in the human race.

Girls are presented with three archetypes of femininity—the Princess, the Good Girl, and the Bad Girl. All women they encounter in their lives seem to fall into one of these three categories. Few are actually encouraged to feel like princesses, and even fewer are treated as princesses, but every girl has seen images of princesses to identify with, whether a popular girl in class, a more glamorous sister, or a movie star. The Princess deserves special attention, magic, and romance. She is the prize men fight for, waiting, beautifully and graciously, on her pedestal, at the end of the rainbow.

The Good Girl is Cinderella, who, if there were any justice in the world, deserves to be the Princess, but never is. She is always busy taking care of the queen and the king, and the other princess and prince. She is much too self-effacing to be able to bear life on the pedestal. She's busy scrubbing the pot for the men to put their gold in. Of course, the men won't even notice her, or see how shiny the pot is as they pick up the gold and present it proudly to the Princess·on the pedestal.

Finally, the Bad Girl is whatever girls are not supposed or allowed to be. She neither cleans nor waits. She grabs for that pot of gold herself, often self-destructively and always unsuccessfully. But her attempts are both distasteful and alarming. She is everything girls are warned about, everything we secretly desire but are much too afraid to go after. She will not end well, and she pays for her sins all along, but she enjoys her pleasures while they last.

So as women we hope to be princesses, but can't really pull it off, thinking we should be good girls, but falling short, wishing to be bad girls, but being too scared. No woman grows up feeling sufficiently feminine.

The Good Girl, then, is an archetype. Some women are more closely modeled on her than others, but most of us have some of her characteristics. (Almost no one is unmitigatedly a good girl because it is impossible; the internal contradictions of femininity are too powerful.) The Good Girl is supposed to be altruistic, selfless, almost exclusively concerned with others but never authoritative or bossy. She is attractive but never proud, steadfast, painstaking, and infinitely reliable, but never comes on strong. Her responses to almost anything are based on feelings rather than naked, cold rationality, and her ways of coping with her small share of turf are gently cooperative and helpful, never competitive or assertive.

The most outstanding characteristic of the Good Girl is the way she relates to others. She is altruistic, selfless, and concerned. She works hard, cares, and comes through. She has to walk a fine line between altruism and influence: she can be everywhere, working, arranging, making organizational miracles happen, but she should not get too much credit. Credit leads to authority. She can be helpful, but never authoritative. She demurs even when she knows much more than anyone else in the room, and knows that everyone else knows that too. She is forever modest, never brags. She is competent, but almost apologetically so. She always seems surprised (and maybe a little pleased) when things work out. If she ever takes full credit, or becomes aware of the extent of her contribution, she immediately shrinks back guiltily. It's like getting muscles from exercise when she was only trying to "reduce." It's unfeminine to be authoritative. So if, in the course of all that unbridled altruism, she starts to feel a little cocky—acting as though she knows what she's doing, taking the initiative without even pretending to ask for advice or permission or at least another opinion, she is considered invasive. She is accused of taking over, of being on an ego trip, of being sexually frustrated. She is told she would be better off at home: She's just an interference. True, she does a lot of tedious work, but her efforts are hardly worth it if she's going to complain or make assumptions and take over. She is very annoying and a little pathetic. The trouble is she doesn't know her place. She embarrasses others who wish she would just shut up and let those who know do it right. She *is* pushy. If she were a man, she would be called authoritative. But there is nothing intrinsically wrong with an authoritative man; on the contrary, there is something wrong with a man who can't command authority. There is, however, something incredibly wrong with an invasive woman. She is the mom on whom everyone can blame their hangups. She is nurturance that suffocates. Children have to be rescued from her clutches. None of us want to be like that, yet we all recognize some part of ourselves in her. She is a woman struggling for a way to be visible.

So the Good Girl is altruistic without being invasive in the ways she relates to others. She is good and kind, and she is also supposed to be attractive. That is, she is supposed to make the best of her physical attributes because nobody likes to look at a homely or sloppy woman, even if she is being efficient and responsible while being looked at. She is neat, clean, pleasant looking if not beautiful, wholesome, and natural. She takes good care of herself physically, not because she is vain, but because she wants to please others. She does research and spends time, money, and thought on not "letting herself go." A good girl never lets herself go—in any way. Her clothes are appropriate and tasteful but not flashy. She plans her wardrobe carefully so that it will never be out of place or embarrassing for anyone else, but does not invest any real attention in style or elegance. If it doesn't come naturally, she modestly withdraws from the beauty competition.

She must be careful not to show any pride in her appearance. Pride is for men. Women who exhibit signs of pride are considered vain. No one condemns their vanity too much because women are known to be relatively superficial in those ways, crying over a broken fingernail. (A man isn't supposed to cry even when he breaks an arm or leg.) But a really good girl is "deeper" than that. She likes to look nice, of course, especially in ways that give pleasure to her loved ones, but she is not vain. She does not enjoy her looks. In fact, she is as inevitably surprised that people find her attractive as that she ends up being competent, even though she works hard at both. She sometimes, at moments of closeness, wistfully admits that she would like to look more glamorous, but she knows she could never pull it off. Even if she had the looks, which she doubts, she is much too shy to flaunt them the way you have to when you're being glamorous. At best, she has the Ivory Look, clean and lovable. But she knows all the flaws in her body. She uses many products to keep herself clean, but not a lot of visible makeup. She takes care of her health more than her looks. She pays attention to her body in order to please others, not to enjoy herself or the attention it might bring her. She diets, exercises, and covers the grey in her hair so she won't offend others, but never for her own pleasure.

So the Good Girl is modestly altruistic, "naturally" attractive, and ready to put anyone else's interests above her own. In relation to the world, she is enduring. This appealing, competent woman also acts like a doormat, a martyr, a passive victim of circumstances always beyond her control. She endures. She does not fight back or even complain. She protests only for others, never for herself. She endures and endures. She can suffer day after day with a smiling face. She can be dying of pain and never show it except for a little pallor. The sad face of her victimization makes us putty in her hands; she is a saint. She has suffered so much, but is willing to suffer more for someone else's sake. She cannot escape unnecessary suffering, because that would be considering the angles, paying attention to her own welfare, and she can't focus on herself that much. What others admire about her is the very fact that she *never* thinks of her own comfort or safety. She is willing to step into the front lines of a violent political demonstration for a good cause, then go back to headquarters with a bloody head to make coffee for the guys, who are debriefing each other.

This woman who can bear anything, who is indomitable when it comes to suffering, does not experience her endurance as strength or think of herself as strong, powerful, or anything that active. If she does, if she ever boasts about her endurance, if she gets a little macho about it, she is both beaten back down (with disapproval, if nothing else) and accused of being a masochist. If she takes any credit, responsibility, or cognizance of her strength, and exhibits any positive feelings about that aspect of herself, she is considered sick. Masochistic means she likes her suffering, that she asked for it, wants it, likes whatever they dish out to her, so it's O.K. to keep on doing it. They're practically doing her a favor by oppressing her. She enjoys it. That active enjoyment of herself is a problem for others: It is too sexual, too assertive. The notion that she might even take enough responsibility for her life to seek out whatever endurance tests she passes is what makes her so suspect. A male athlete endures hours of pain and boredom to get into shape. That's all right; he is just doing what he wants to do, following his inclination. A woman who takes pride in her ability to endure is unfeminine and peculiar.

This selfless, attractive martyr is consumed with concern, worry, and empathy. Her response to everything is highly emotional, but never theatrical. When she speaks about the state of the world, her voice is filled with pain. She suffers with and for those more unfortunate than she, and is deeply and personally moved when she sees evidence of injustice. But she also cries about the bad haircut she got while hurrying between appointments. She cries, or almost cries, about everything. Tears well up at the slightest provocation. She swallows them bravely. Occasionally she breaks down and sobs, but then quickly pulls herself together, apologizes, dabs her eyes, and gets back to work. Of course, tears keep welling up while she works. She worries endlessly about her children, her coworkers, her family, her neighbors, her animals, her plants. She worries and worries and suffers and suffers and carries on in her quiet way.

If she carries on too noticeably, insisting on her right to expression, insisting she has reason to be upset and that her upset should be taken seriously and attended to (rather than just induce a little guilt in those around her who aren't nearly as sensitive), she is considered hysterical. She *should* suffer but not require any attention from anyone. When her suffering interferes in any way, she is considered out of control, hysterical. A hysterical woman is not an evil woman (women are known to become hysterical easily due to hormones), but she is a drag and a bit of a joke. Others roll their eyes and shrug when they talk about a hysterical woman. There's no talking to her, no reasoning with her. She cries and yells and carries on like a baby with diaper rash. Of course, if there *is* any reasoning with her, if she listens to reason, or even uses reason to discuss her responses, she is no longer feminine. A rational woman is a hard-on, a cold fish, forever intellectualizing. A rational woman is an anomaly, and also a very unappealing creature. She is barren and unnatural. A woman who does not respond primarily and almost exclusively with emotions is a woman who has no feelings. A woman without feelings is a travesty of nature. Women are supposed to be all feeling.

Finally, this good girl who responds to everything heart first, with tears in her eyes, copes with life in a totally cooperative manner. She is helpful, nonassertive, never asks for credit, applauds everyone else's ideas, and makes people work without letting on that she had anything to do with it. She always defers to experts, even when there are none present. She cites experts, even if she has to invent them. She would never presume to speak for herself because she might be wrong. She is totally self-effacing about her work. She must work all the time, but she should never be seen working too hard—that makes people uncomfortable and guilty, so she must do all her work with a smile, with ease, with grace. She does boring work with a song in her heart and a smile on her lips, a walking "have a good day" button. She likes nothing better than pleasing others, so if it pleases them to exploit her, she lets them do it without protest.

If she doesn't like it, she is considered competitive, which is not very attractive in a woman. She is not supposed to want to win, get credit for her effort, or excel. Virtue and her family's health are her only reward. A competitive woman is probably sick; she might even suffer from penis envy. A woman who suffers from penis envy is pathetic. Because she can never have a penis, she will always be inferior. If she doesn't accept that inferiority with good grace she is not a good girl. A good girl never plays to win. She lets others win, pretending to know less than they do. When something is explained to her, she pretends to understand slowly, then gives the explainer all the credit for getting through to her slow and sieve-like mind.

So the Good Girl is supposed to cooperate, but not too efficiently. She is not meant to be a full partner, a collaborator, just a helper. When she acts incompetent, as if she didn't know how to do anything, as if you could explain the simplest instructions to her over and over, and she still couldn't get them right, if she pays no real attention to how things are done, she is called vague. A Good Girl is never too sure of anything, of course, so she is considered vague. Since she responds with her heart rather than her head, she may be intense, but functionally vague. You never know why she says what she says and does what she does. It's kind of cute, kind of lovable; she's so unpredictable. It makes her no threat at all, even if she's often a bit of a wet blanket and a burden. She makes others feel a little guilty because she is so good, and she isn't much fun, because that would require something other than martyrdom. But she is what makes the world go round.

So that's the Good Girl in action—in all of us. We may rebel against our inclination to be good, or regret that we can't be better than we are, but there is no getting away from the Good Girl as a standard. We see her everywhere. She is a cultural archetype with a long history. She is Iphigenia, the young innocent ready for sacrifice, or the Virgin Mary (whose boundless purity is rewarded by seeing her son die young, but for a good cause), pure enough to bear the son who will save the world. The range of the Good Girl is relatively narrow, variations on a theme. The message is always the same: Be good enough and you may be sacrificed on a really important altar, unless providence saves you for marriage, in which case your goodness will bear fruit in the splendor of your children's lives. The Good Girl is the innocent whose virtue is rewarded with ever more ennobling suffering. Her prince may come, but she is in a lot of trouble before and after his arrival.

She is held up as a model, a noble ideal, someone young girls dream of becoming. The pure young thing who never loses her hopeful friendliness even when people hurt and deprive her. She goes through trials, tribulations, and ordeals, but her essential worth is eventually recognized by a wonderful man, who marries her and puts her on a pedestal, and for whom she bears beautiful children who love her deeply. The story may end vaguely around there, and when we pick it up later, she has become the good woman who had only a few moments of love, joy, and fulfillment before her cycle of trials, tribulations, and ordeals started again. Her man may go off to war, be killed or crippled by some villain, leave her while under the spell of a bad girl who seduced him, or earn a living on the road, and she has to spend her adult life waiting for him, mourning him, or enshrining him. Her only joy is seeing the children grow. She inspires her sons to greatness and gratitude. They go off and achieve greatness, and, for the ultimate happy ending, she gets to see a sign of their triumphs on her deathbed.

Soap operas on television tell her story. She is an ideal *and* a norm. The airwaves are full of her. Mary Tyler Moore's character, Mary Richards, is a wonderful example of her "normalcy." She is not a saint and leads a relatively safe, easy life, sheltered from any exotic martyrdom, but she is in almost continual anxiety, worry, fear, upset, or concern. She has good times too, but when they interfere with her worries, she feels guilty. Mary is always ready to pitch in and help out, and must sometimes be gently told not to be quite so helpful because it makes others feel crummy. She is cute and attractive, not glamorous or gorgeous. She works hard for little pay, grateful for the chance. She tries to be objective and rational, but luckily her heart and her instincts lead her every time. She tries to be so nice, so cooperative, that she occasionally screws up because she is too nice, too squeamish or innocent to face the truth of a situation. She is a prude, of course, but wistfully apologetic about it. She is the nice, clean, healthy, all-American Good Girl par excellence, a blueprint for millions of girls growing up watching her. She blushes when she says a word like *darn*.

Mary Richards fits into this culture. She is the mold into which we have all tried to fit to some extent. She is popular at school, rewarded for her good-girl femininity, encouraged in it, held up to us. She is what every institution of the patriarchy is mandated to make us into. "Be a good girl!" is not an empty phrase. Parents and teachers mean it and teach us that it is more important for little girls to get along and be nice to others than to fight for their rights, excel at some discipline, or develop their minds. Little girls who seem too single-minded in their pursuit of any kind of mastery are considered at risk: Without help they become stunted women. Little boys similarly occupied are considered potential geniuses. Girls should be well rounded; boys are urged to specialize.

The general values of the culture, transmitted through art, communications media, and the institutions of the patriarchy from school to the workplace, are the matrix in which we are socialized. The primary site, however, of our feminization is the family. We learn how to be human in the family, how to relate to ourselves, others, and the world. But we learn a different humanity according to whether we are little girls or little boys. We learn to be potential women *or* potential men. The family, especially the nuclear family as we know it, is the arena in which the child struggles to become the kind of human being she or he is being molded into. We have few models, few partners in the struggle, little help. We have one woman, one man, a few other children, and a distant view of older, other people, our relatives and neighbors. They either all adhere to the same view or argue about it in such a way that we know perfectly well there is a right and a wrong way, and it is important to do what is right. Every family has its "black sheep," its failures, its successes, its favorites. We play it out with the extended family as the audience, but we learn it from our immediate, nuclear family. So, if our mandate is to become good little potential women, we look to Mom, who is what we have to become. We also look to Dad, and to older siblings of both genders, and we learn that they have many privileges that will never be ours. It's confusing, but Mom is there as guide and teacher; it's her job, after all, to turn us into good girls.

The mother-daughter relationship is forced to perpetuate the contradictions of femininity. We each make our own peace with the social mandate we have been given and find our own internal accommodation to the strictures imposed on gender by the culture we live in. The mother-daughter relationship shapes and facilitates that accommodation in a particular way. The specific character of each woman's accommodation to the mandate of femininity varies a great deal among different ethnic and class groupings, but we believe that the general structure of femininity outlined in the first chapter holds true as the prototype of femininity in every part of the culture. Each mother has to transmit the rules of femininity to her daughters to help them survive in the world as she knows it. Each daughter has been shaped and colored by the model and dogma of femininity shown by her mother.

Reproduction of the pernicious gender system is deeply necessary for the emotional survival of most mothers, which makes it irresistible to most daughters. The price for not conforming to the gender system is very high. The blame, both for perpetuating it and collaborating in its perpetuation, is often placed on women. But this system is not in our interest, was not designed or allowed to develop with us in mind: It serves men, even if only a small portion of men. We are its victims.

Mothers are required to produce good girls, feminine, heterosexual daughters. The daughters have to be ready and willing to ally themselves exclusively with someone they have been taught to see as hopelessly "other" (heterosexuality), to internalize all the limitations of cultural inferiority (femininity), and to exhibit the symptoms of this complex, punitive struggle in a prescribed way, with lighthearted compliance. It is no easy matter to get a healthy, lively girl child to accept that fate. It takes work, dedication, and the weight of centuries of culture. Mothers are at the front lines of this war of sexual imperialism.

As mothers, we are in a terrible bind. We are put into a position of false omnipotence by getting all the praise and blame for what our children become. We can only be "good mothers" if we turn out "good daughters," those who obey, follow, and accept their inferior status. Mothers are called upon to make sure innocent girl infants become emotionally crippled, helpless, incomplete without a man, and to accept sole responsibility for the results. If a daughter becomes the Marie Osmond doll who can't stand up without being supported by the Donny Osmond doll (who stands splendidly on his own, and is additionally capable of holding up his sister), her mother has made her so. If a daughter fails to become crippled by femininity, Mom has produced a freak. A daughter who rebels is monstrous, the product of a clearly—though perhaps surreptitiously—monstrous mother, a castrating bitch, a ball-crusher, a witch, or a dyke. So even though women are asked to accept the notion that the state of passive femininity is "natural" to us, mothers are blamed if this natural process does not occur.

The mother is supposed to "control" her children, both overtly and subliminally. "Don't let her wear that blue snowsuit; it might turn her into a tomboy in later life!" She has to keep track at all times. "Don't let her eat what she wants; she will become self-indulgent and fat and no man will want to marry her." The price of femininity is more than constant vigilance, however: It is constant suppression, repression, and deprivation. Never a hair or a nasty feeling out of place. The daughter is the mother's product. The mother is judged, her basic humanity evaluated, on the basis of her daughter's neatness, sweetness, and docility. Growing, living children are not naturally neat, sweet, or docile. They like to grow, expand, explore, taste, try, destroy to see what happens, spit and fart and shit and belch. They are not naturally dainty. But a mother who cannot make her daughter appear dainty at all times is a bad mother. A good mother, in addition, should rarely have to resort to overt censure and punishment. She should have the ability to convey them with only a look, which she can do if she has managed to convince her growing daughter that a mother's feelings of sorrow and disappointment when she is not a perfect little angel are more vital than the daughter's desires and needs. So the mother not only has an impossible task to do, she is also required to do it in an impossible manner. She has to prevent any occurrence of rebellion or autonomy because such attitudes directly contradict femininity. Confronting rebellion, as she does with her son, is a way of permitting but channeling it. A rebellious daughter is considered to have had faulty gender training and to be the product of a suspect mother.

Since our daughters make us successful mothers, we strive to turn out slightly better versions of ourselves, hoping our daughters will choose the same lifestyle but manage it even more impeccably, invisibly, ingratiatingly, femininely. It is all right with us if a daughter has a slightly more successful husband whom she pleases more often, prettier children, a nicer home. Differences in lifestyle and attitude threaten and challenge us as mothers. The angry feminist daughter and the glamorous career woman challenge a mother's hard-won acceptance of her limitations. Such daughters could upset the whole apple cart: If it's O.K. for them to be free, equal, sexual, and pushy, why not for us?

To be good at mothering, the only job women have been given to validate our lives, we have to subject our daughters to the same crushing restraints we were subjected to, an injustice we wish we could avoid. We promise to be better mothers than our mothers were, and what we mean by that—before we have children—is that we won't act like conventional mothers at all. We will encourage our daughters to be free, courageous, do whatever they want, even if they become rebels or outcasts: It beats becoming drudges like our own mothers were. We have the best intentions. But we don't realize that intentions are merely conscious. A number of powerful but usually unconscious psychodynamics are at work and propel us in the same direction as our mothers. Mothers are good girls grown up, trying to be "good" mothers.

Women come into motherhood with unfulfilled needs for mothering of our own. Most of us have had what psychoanalysts call "inadequate mothering." As infants, we need our mothers to be totally available to us, ready to meet our every need, and to reflect back to us our every feeling. We need our mothers to be warm, loving, soothing, nurturing extensions of ourselves. We need not to be forced to recognize too early, before we are developmentally ready, that she is another, separate human being, with firm boundaries and a life of her own over which we have no control and which doesn't include or concern us. It is from this safe haven of total access that we can slowly grow, at our own pace, into the world. We come and go, and Mom is always there to welcome us back, to praise and comfort us, and to provide the sustenance we need to explore further. And slowly, as we become better able to take care of our own needs, we can afford to recognize the enormous distance and separateness between ourselves and our life-line mothers.

Most of us were forced to recognize this distance too early. Our mothers had concerns, struggles, feelings of their own that had nothing much to do with us, but we had no way of knowing that. What we learned was that the warm, cozy, nourishing maternal envelope was not always there, not always warm or cozy or nourishing. We didn't get the chance to discover our own boundaries slowly and with safety. We got confused. We felt warm and then cold, hungry and then satisfied, but the source of comfort was not always there when we needed her. We had, at first, no way of distinguishing between her nurturing and our needs. We learn that slowly, as we take charge of our own bodies and begin to recognize what is us and what is not us. When mother is not available enough, we are not in a position to explore the us and the not-us. We can only yearn and want and cry and despair, and then feel some relief when the nurturer returns. So if we grow up with inadequate or ambivalent mothering, we develop a confused sense of our own boundaries. We're never quite sure where we leave off and our mothers begin, or where they leave off and we are ourselves.

When we become mothers, we want to merge with our daughters as we never could with our own mothers. We want them to be the other half of us, the warm extension we longed for. We have trouble recognizing our daughters as separate human beings, separate from us, their mothers. We answer questions for them long after they can speak, assuming they feel about things as we do, that they want what we want for them. We are surprised and displeased when they have different opinions. We believe that, as the result of the nurturance and care we give our girl children, there will be a sunset into which we will walk together. Since we become so symbiotically identified with our daughters, we are likely to have a hard time letting them go, or letting them define their own boundaries, when they need to. We can't let them go because we're not through with them—we still need them.

We treat our sons differently, considering efforts to stop them from too much exploration, too much risk taking and moving out on their own, too much self-definition even to the point of danger understandable but mistaken. We may want to merge with our sons, but we are helped, by the whole culture, to let go gently, tearfully, but definitely. Mothers must let sons go to war. We must let them grow up and sow their wild oats, make their own mistakes, and assume responsibility for their own lives. Mothers who don't are castraters.

But mothers have to prevent daughters from all such explorations. We are allowed to indulge our own symbiotic needs and keep our daughters closely tied to us. They become feminine that way, and we are considered good mothers as a result. When a daughter spends all her time with her mother, they are considered close in a positive way, as long as both pay adequate lip service and real service to a man. When a son spends all his time with his mother, he is considered a mama's boy. A dutiful son loves his mother, tries to take care of her, but feels rather uncomfortable and awkward in her presence. It's a little claustrophobic, too close, too connected. He breathes a small sigh of relief when he leaves her, opens his collar, and sprinkles a little profanity into his conversation to reestablish his freedom and masculinity.

Most of us resented the freedom our brothers, friends' brothers, or male cousins enjoyed while girls were urged to cool it, keep it in, and sit on it. We resented our mothers for being the enforcers, the ones who seemed to care most that we act ladylike and feminine. Men seemed to enjoy it, every now and then, when we were a little wild. Mom was always the one who called a halt, who looked worried and censorious. So when the time comes to deal with our own daughters, we have mixed feelings. We want them to have some of the freedoms we never had, to have them for us, in fact. And yet, when we see the inevitable consequences of such explorations of freedom, when our daughters show any sign of "masculinity," we are frightened and pull back, partly because it threatens our good-mother image, but mostly because we are not ready to give up the hope of merging with our daughters and are afraid we will be abandoned if they "go too far." There is much less hope for merging with wild, individuated, eccentric, freedom-loving individuals than there is with good girls (or boys) who stay close to home and take an interest in our interests. So we pull back and act inconsistent. We're either cheering on our daughters or telling them to stop. We end up confusing them even more, giving them even less to go on when they try to define who they are and who we are.

The need for symbiosis is not felt by girls alone. But girls are encouraged to seek out symbiotic ties in their familial relationships, to merge with their husbands and children when they grow up, not to seek success and glory out in the world. They are asked to find fulfillment in their mothering role, not in their mastery of the world. Men can marry the mother they never had enough of. Women have to *be* the mother before they have had her, be the mother and never have her—and hope some day to create in their daughters a mother for themselves.

The better the girl we are, the more we are forced to collaborate in the cycle of oppression that binds us to our mothers and our daughters. We model goodness for our daughters, demand their self-suppression, guilt-trip them for any attempt to break out, to be "bad." Partly, we worry that they will come to no good end (which might be preferable for some), that they will suffer more than they have to, more than we did. Partly we envy their increased freedom, but our goodness does not permit us to face that envy, to work it through and encourage our enviable daughters on their paths. We are not supposed to feel that way, so we try not to, and instead of feeling the envy and dealing with it, we act it out on our daughters. We suffer "for them," thus making it absolutely impossible for them to take any risks. It's hard enough for a daughter to go against an entire culture, a way of life, even if she has supportive parents and is responsible only to herself. But it is impossible when her mother's health and happiness rest on her not doing anything risky.

Sometimes, when our daughters break out successfully, achieving goals we have wanted for ourselves, we have no choice but to incorporate our daughters' successes, eating them up and taking them over. It's a way to make success O.K., to reduce cognitive dissonance. We decide what's all right and what's over the line, keeping the true criteria a secret from our daughters. We are inscrutably pleased or disappointed by them, often wounded that they do not consult us or at least read our everchanging minds before acting. We restate our daughters' intentions in some adventure in a way acceptable to us, thus giving our daughters the impression that their achievements were no big deal and, in fact, were expected of them. "Why, dear, I always knew you could do it! A nice girl like you can do almost anything she sets her mind to, and without being any less feminine." At other times, we take away the glory by being so relieved, so released from the terrible worry we suffered when the project was in process (or now realize we might have suffered had we known about it), that it hardly seems worth it to our daughters anymore. Their risky and interesting adventures have to be kept secret because they are not openly acceptable to us.

Sometimes we are deeply hurt by a daughter's silence, by her unwillingness to share her life, by her lies or evasive answers to questions, or by her flying off the handle and accusing us of meddling. We don't understand how the tension built up or how a rift developed. But as soon as she tells us anything we don't want to hear, we censor or we criticize. We want to think of ourselves as good mothers, as understanding mothers, as mothers a daughter can come to with any problem, not like our own mothers, who were much too uptight about certain subjects like sexuality or career goals. We understand the undermining effects of criticism. We are modern women, emancipated and realistic, wanting to prepare our daughters to live in the present, not in the past. But in actual conversations with our daughters, something happens. We hear ourselves turning into our own mothers. We give opinions that make no sense to us either, but know they are right under the circumstances. We remember how we felt about the way our mothers treated us, how we really felt (of course we loved them, and they had very hard lives, but they did drive us crazy much of the time). So we try to resolve the tension by telling our daughters how much better we are to them than our mothers were to us, how lucky they are to have us, not their grandmas, as mothers. We give them a very strange message: "Become like me, even though I am insisting on all the ways I did not become like my mother."

Our relationships with our own mothers become the battleground on which our struggles with our daughters are carried out. The grandmother is the audience, the judge, the standard, the nemesis, the phantom player, whether she ever interferes or not, before and after death. She taught the roles of mother and daughter. We may try, this time around, to play the ideal mothers we wished for, but we need our daughters' approbation to fulfill the fantasy of perfect mother-daughter bonding. That puts a lot of pressure on our daughters. We may wish to give our daughters all the material things we wanted, which would permit us to satisfy a child part of ourselves in some belated way. But then we end up feeling entitled to prescribe their lives and identities for them. "Be like me, want what I wanted, and stay with me." Or we may simply imitate our mothers' mothering, on the assumption that they were good mothers, that what was good enough for us and our mothers is good enough for our daughters.

But then we must be prepared to see mirror versions of ourselves grow up and turn into girls with problems that remind us of our own. We have to accept the idea that we are a part of an endless chain of women just like ourselves, that differences grow out of chance happenings, that we have no control over events, that women just flow and endure. We have to be prepared to feel that mothering is "natural," that we are all we could and should be. Some of us might be prepared to make all those assumptions philosophically, but accepting them psychologically requires profound resignation, total passivity, and a form of depression based on the conviction that we are helpless victims. After all, we are not raising proud champions whose calling is to subdue and cultivate the universe, but an endless chain of "good girls."

Television's Mary Richards from now to eternity might not seem like such a bad idea to everyone, but Mary Richards would be a far less appealing ideal were she not surrounded and nourished by a cast of supporting characters who are not "right." Mary among Marys is boring, stifling, a wilted flower. In real life, a good girl like Mary is hardly ever an associate producer in a small news station, a position that brings the world right into her lap and asks only that she respond. In reality, a Mary would have to become totally assertive, totally unlike herself to win Mary's prizes. A real, live Mary Richards can be very depressed, sometimes taking pills to preserve her equanimity, and occasionally being hospitalized if the depression becomes too severe. She usually survives, but the image of an endless chain of self-effacing women smiling their way through painful life crises into a pleasant, feminine grave is a lot less appealing than the picture of spunky Mary Richards struggling to get the news out in Minneapolis generation after generation.

A woman can play the mother role a few different ways, but unless the job and the status of mothering change completely, she cannot do it well. She is tied to her daughter in a way that enforces femininity. The sacrificial mother teaches her daughter altruism and emotionalism, showing her, with the best of intentions, that grown up women live only for others, as Mom does.

Mom's reward is love, and, however expressed, it has to be her sustenance. The burden placed on the daughter is enormous and two-fold: She has to accept getting nothing but love in her adult life, thereby renouncing excitement, pleasure, freedom and mastery, and she has to furnish her mother's emotional sustenance in her present life. In other words, she has to feed her mother now and her children (and husband) later in a complex chain of self-sacrifice followed by supposedly self-chosen sacrifice for others.

The over-compensating mother squelches her daughter's development by her confusion between what she wants to give and what her daughter needs. Mother teaches daughter to cooperate with a vengeance, to give up completely and let Mom run the show. The traditional mother teaches her daughter a kind of endurance. This is the way it is and always has been and always will be. Learn to go with it. This is your lot in life, learn to live with it. This is what it's like for women.

The effect of this restricted set of roles on daughters varies, depending on a great number of factors. It is vastly overdetermined. But some kind of continuum of femininity can be described, even if sketchily. Each effect is actually "normal," that is, a part of acceptable femininity. When taken to a greater extreme, the capacity to endure, for example, becomes much more evidently self-destructive.

As daughters, we can easily feel worthless. We suffer from low self-esteem, from poor self-image and feel bad about ourselves because our mothers modeled worthlessness for us. They put up with being treated like mere women, then let it happen to us, never defending us against our brothers or fathers. They accepted inferior status, which tells us something: There is something wrong with women, and that's why we are treated badly. If nothing were wrong with us, we wouldn't allow such treatment. The fact that we allow it means that we deserve it. We really are inferior (men would never allow it), and we are to blame. We see it in our mothers and are angry at them. They are clearly depressed and long-suffering, so we have to feel sorry for them and stop being angry (we are their only sustenance), which depresses us. We act depressed, mopey, dull, teary, and we are treated like drones, which is another, further blow to our flagging self-esteem. We realize that there is an explanation: We really are worth very little; it's our fault. If we were different . . . We join our mothers.

When we don't join them, when we find a way to disregard the message, to feel good about ourselves, to glory in some triumph or brag (quietly to ourselves) about some skill or accomplishment, we immediately start to feel we are betraying our mothers. Our good feelings become a question of loyalty. Feeling good is treason because it means we have not become totally identified with our mothers' constant suffering, their victimization in all its myriad forms. We have the nerve to differentiate ourselves from our mothers, to decide we might just make it out of the family and into the world. We decide to go for the individual solution, just to enjoy our own lives rather than validate or extend our mothers'. We step away from the army of victims and declare ourselves survivors. Momentarily, we declare the war over. That is selfish. It is leaving Mother in the ditch to carry the blues all by herself, exploiting her martyrdom merely to have a good time. And it makes us anxious, so we either find some way to cut the enjoyment short ("O.K., Mom, I had a nice outing, but now I'm back. I wouldn't want to overdo it and get addicted to freedom.") or to end it with a disaster so as to prove, once again, that fun doesn't pay (as Mom warned).

One way to ensure a disastrous ending or follow-up, if all else fails, is to tell our mothers about the good times we had. They are sure to disapprove, to feel betrayed (or abandoned or left out or envious), and to sound critical or disappointed in us. And we need their approval. We are merged with our mothers, unseparated, not yet fully expelled from the womb. Mothers teach us this too, both by the way they mother us (inevitably inadequately, given the choices), which doesn't provide enough of a safety zone to risk total, cold-turkey separation, and by the way they pull us back into the symbiotic cocoon, hoping to finally merge with their own mothers'. So, if we aren't quite sure which one we are, mother's mother or mother's daughter, our mothers' cues give us most of our directions: Mothers are our other half. They tell us who we are and whether it's all right to be that way. Their disapproval raises serious self-doubt. We are afraid of losing them altogether. They know better, have known longer, have seen it all. They have suffered for us and we repay them by becoming creatures unworthy of their love. Disagreeing with them, approving someone or something they do not, is impossible. It is only possible to be ambivalent. We are what they think, not just what we think. We may decide to rebel and to risk the loss of their approval, but that means closing off any hope of merging, of never again being mothers' good little girls whom they love and take care of. That's a serious risk and an incredibly high price to pay for doing something that should be encouraged by our nurturers, invariably the very same mothers who exact the price.

Femininity, then, is a program, a mode of behavior that ensures that the cycle of oppression will continue for women. It comes in a few versions, but all of them serve to bind us to our oppression. The most common, most revered version of femininity is the Good Girl, who is altruistic, attractive, enduring, emotional, and cooperative. She doesn't want anything and she never fights back. She is a doll—a working doll, a robot, a "Stepford wife." That means she is, since she really is a human being underneath that Stepford makeup and mind control, one-sided, underdeveloped, unskilled, and stunted. She only responds to the world, never acts on it. She becomes a mother, a woman who has been promised, throughout years of terrible emotional deprivation, that someday she will find happiness in her daughter. She needs her daughter and exploits her by necessity in the struggle to grow up herself and to heal the wounds of her battle for survival with her own mother. The daughter grows up feeling worthless, terrified of freedom, and desperately in need of her mother's love and approval. She has been turned into another feminine woman, another good girl who will put up and shut up and smile.

3
DADDY'S GIRL
The Father-Daughter Relationship

The present gender system requires women to turn to men for validation of their femininity. To play according to the rules, women must learn the importance of men, putting their needs first and accepting their opinions as the Law. Women must learn to participate in ritual interactions that affirm and reproduce male superiority and female inferiority, their masculinity and our femininity. Women must learn to defer to men's wishes, postpone our own gratification, and never demand more than men are willing to give. In spite of our desires to act for ourselves we must learn to accept male authority and the limits of subversion. The task for all daughters is to become heterosexual women who love men more than themselves.

We come to understand the nature of gender relations in interaction with our fathers. He encourages us to be the kind of girl men will love, the woman who is fragile, helpless, ineffectual, sensitive, and catty. Dad rewards our compliance with affection and approval but withdraws that love when we show signs of becoming too self-directed or autonomous. The limits of our power are defined by the boundaries of his tolerance for rebellion. His love for us is secure as long as we do as he says and let him take care of us. As he shows us what men can do for the women they love, he prepares a place for men in our hearts.

As a man and a father, he represents and is invested in maintaining the patriarchal status quo. The family is the arena in which he may act out the privileges given to men by virtue of their gender. No matter where he stands in the ranked order of men, at home he is the King and rules with a sense of entitlement and authority. He wants from his daughter what he wants from women in general—obedience, respect, deference, and love. If we can deliver this gift to him willingly and passionately, he promises to help us deal with the dangers of the world and

41

the choices that we confront. If we can demonstrate to his satisfaction that we are devoted to his will and his pleasure, we can
feel better about ourselves and better able to withstand the
deprivations of our socially ascribed powerlessness.

The daughter's first important relationship with a man is
with her father because with him she feels a love that is special,
because he is special. Overvalued in the world and idealized in
the home, the father promises his daughter a share of that aura
of strength and capability that is reserved only for men. If the
daughter can be the kind of girl that he wants her to be, she
can feel special too — the silent partner in a ritual of romance
tinged with secrecy and taboo.

The father-daughter relationship played out under the
watchful gaze of the mother is the first mystification of heterosexuality. Whether he is a devil or a saint, a Milquetoast or a
monster, a tyrant or a baby, the daughter falls for him because
he is there and he is unique. The daughter learns that men are
"special" by observing the ways her mother treats her father.
The rules and rituals of proper gender demeanor are acted out
before the daughter's eyes and she learns that he should be
deferred to, since he is the king of his castle. To insure heterosexual harmony, she must anticipate his needs and meet them
efficiently and cheerfully, considering his likes and dislikes first
in the daily routine of family life. The mother is the daughter's
first example of feminine submission to male authority.

Mother cautions the daughter not to interrupt her father,
not to bother him when he wants to relax, not to ask too many
questions when he makes a pronouncement, not to defy his
authority. Mother shows the daughter that she understands her
man very well and knows how best to make him happy. This is
both her duty and her privilege, and despite her dissatisfactions
with him, she takes care of this man because she loves him,
because it gives her pleasure, because he is a man.

The daughter is aware that her mother is not always happy
in her role as the father's loyal servant and administrator. Her
mother often complains to her that he is not making enough
money, doesn't take her anywhere, or is as demanding as a

baby. But she always adds that he must be respected because he is, after all, her husband and the daughter's father. She defends his right to discipline and punish because he is the ultimate voice of authority and reason in the household. She claims that she cannot intervene, influence, or control his desires to maintain order, judge, or punish. She shows the daughter through her silence or ineffectual arguments that she is helpless to stop the father from acting out his power. She defends his privilege even when she says she suffers under its exercise. Despite her own dissatisfactions, she instructs the daughter in appropriate heterosexual deference.

The mother also protects the father's image, telling her daughter she is lucky to have a father who is "good," who doesn't abuse his power in despotic ways. She compares him with men who beat their children, never speak to them, drink, curse, or run out on their families. She praises the father for his control in restraining himself from acts of cruelty that men are often famous for. Even though her husband may be more gentle than most, he is a "real" man, and therefore deserves her respect and obedience.

The daughter observes that in times of family crisis the mother seeks to protect her "protector." It appears that her mother really knows how fragile he is, incapable of handling the emotional stresses of illness, death, divorce, or life's other upheavals. Conspiratorially the mother whispers to the daughter, "Don't tell your father, it might kill him," "Let's just keep this between us girls; your father just can't handle things like that." Mom excuses Dad's anxieties, his vulnerabilities, and his sometimes disguised insecurities, as she presents him to her daughter in the light of valued masculinity, a man as he should be.

Concluding that men can be both tyrants and babies, the daughter learns that men should never be betrayed, exposed, hurt, or angered by the women who love them, one part of the heterosexual heritage used to ensure successful relations with men. And the daughter learns that having a man, no matter what his defects, is better than having no man to call your own.

By watching her parents carefully, the daughter learns the

limits of feminine willfulness, the possibilities of subversion, and the rewards for compliance. If her mother's tactics work, the daughter may test her mother's rules for herself. Yet, because he is not her husband but her father, she wants him to treat her differently. In competition with her mother for his attention and affection, the daughter hopes to have a different relationship to him, perhaps one that is more loving and less authoritarian. Although her mother has declared him as her personal domain, which she often protects with tenacity and jealousy, the daughter tries to hold his attention and receive the affection that her mother seems to be denied. She would like to try her luck with the tyrant/baby. She wants to be Daddy's Girl.

When the daughter turns toward her father she is seeking support for her individuality and autonomy, aspects of her self that her mother seems less willing or able to validate. She hopes that an alliance with him will clarify the fuzzy boundaries between her and his Other Woman (his wife). He stands for Otherness, for difference, and for autonomy, and she thinks that with him as a friend, the confusing and often angry relationship with her mother will become less central in her life.

The mother seems to notice her only when she wants something done, or when she is displeased with the daughter's behavior. She is often too busy to listen to the daughter's stories or problems. Because her role of nurturer and caretaker of all family members is so demanding she takes her daughter's demands for attention as another interruption of daily schedule. The daughter doesn't understand why her mother isn't more interested in her but concludes that perhaps it is because girls aren't that interesting, or that she prefers boys and men.

As she turns from her mother to her father for attention and approval, the daughter decides that pleasing her father is more important anyway, since he is the only really special parent in the family. If she can get and keep his love, then perhaps she can share some of his specialness and be spared the consequences of her ascribed inferiority. If he recognizes her and gives her some of his precious time, the daughter feels chosen, elevated from the ordinary lot of womanhood, made more visible, lovable, and alive.

Following her mother's example, she too awaits his return each evening, hoping for some time with him alone. She wants him to defend her against the tyranny of her mother and the boredom of domestic life. He represents the excitement and importance of the nondomestic world of men, and his arrival home changes the mundane to the marvelous. She watches as her mother sets out to please him with food, service, and special attention to his problems and concerns. She listens in rapt attention as he tells about his day, which sounds much more interesting than the one that she has had at home with the mother. She looks forward to the time when she can do some of these things for him, when she can receive his praise for being the kind of girl he likes. Even though he sometimes seems gruff and distant, the daughter seeks to show him that she can make things more pleasant for him. If he will let her, she will prove her loyalty to him.

Her own dissatisfaction with the world she and her mother inhabit, full of repetitive tasks and boredom, helps place her father in a romantic light. The power and authority accorded him as a man are stunning but, she believes, justly deserved. His scarcity at home and his commitment to the world make her time with him more precious. She feels she can go to him for the Truth since he seems to know so much and is so sure of his opinions. She respects his rationality, his knowledge, and his interests and hopes he will share them with her so she can feel more secure, better able to make choices and carry them through. He seems to encourage her independence, take her questions seriously, and be pleased when she turns to him for advice and assistance.

The daughter listens as he holds forth on the state of the world and marvels at his knowledge. At the dinner table he speaks in a confident manner about realms she perceives only dimly. Her mother doesn't say much as she moves back and forth from the kitchen to the table, seeing that the butter is there, the glasses filled, and the plates refilled, but he sits there, larger than life, expounding on topics of importance while she sits in silence, wondering if she could possibly say anything to win his approval and get recognition.

When her father finally acknowledges that his little girl thinks the way he does, or shares some of his personality traits, he may encourage a relationship that allows his daughter to get closer to him. Even though she is only a girl, he appears to want to usher her into his magical world of masculine interests and activities. He allows her to help wash the car, takes her on walks to buy cigarettes and newspapers, invites her to watch his favorite TV shows with him. The daughter waits for the time to arrive with tense anticipation, hoping that she won't disappoint him because she is not a boy and doesn't know what boys know. She wants to be the best companion she can, since he seems to get so much pleasure from showing her his world.

If their camaraderie is allowed to flourish, if her mother seems pleased by her tie to him, the daughter comes to see her father in a new light; in his frequently distant and often unapproachable authority, she sees the secret dreamer, the poet, or the rebel. The usually forceful and sure voice changes, softening, as he tells her about his life and the events that shaped it.

When Dad shares his "feelings" with her, even if he steps down from his exalted position only once in her life, the daughter cherishes these personal and private exchanges forever. She feels she has elicited his confidence, tiny revelations that her father is "sensitive," perhaps even "tortured," by his own sense of failure in the world of men. He talks to her as if she were a peer, a grown-up; he wants her to know him as he really is, to understand how difficult it is to be a man. Her view of him is radically altered by this shared intimacy, and he is transformed into a romantic hero, a tragic figure who must carry his sadness alone. He may speak of his own father's death, or the career he wanted to have, or the burden of responsibility that has no end. Triumphant and touched by compassion, the daughter now holds her father's new image close; now that she understands him, she vows to make him happy if she can.

Identifying with her father as a victim, the daughter tries to be the kind of girl who will please him, hoping to make up for some of the disappointment he has felt. Even if her mother refuses to see this side of him, or ridicules his "weaknesses," the daughter is convinced that she alone really understands what this man is about. She is not concerned whether he is a good provider, or a man of education, or acts unreasonably, or on occasion cruelly. Now that she knows him better than anyone else, his real or imputed faults make him more precious to her, she has come close to male power and authority and believes that behind the role is a man she can help with love. As her romance with the father-as-victim grows, she dedicates herself to defending him and keeping his secret.

The tragic hero of the daughter's fantasy is forgiven his excesses, and his absences, because she identifies with his sense of confinement and unrealized dreams. Raging silently at her mother for having little sympathy for her romantic hero, the daughter commits her energies to pleasing him; anticipating his needs, meeting his demands; acting as his ally in family disputes. No matter how her mother rails against him, the daughter forgives him his faults and in her heart makes an alliance with men and masculine authority. Now that she knows him she doesn't want to lose him. Being good for him seems a small price to pay for their new relationship.

To be Daddy's Girl, to achieve her place in his heart, the daughter has to work hard at being the kind of daughter he wants her to be. Otherwise the thrilling moments of acceptance and visibility will be overshadowed by his disapproval and anger. When he suddenly becomes silent, removed, she wonders if she has done something to displease him. It feels unbearable to be cast out of his good graces, banished to the barren land of worthlessness and invisibility. His displeasure sets off fears of abandonment and exile, and the daughter seeks to understand what she has done wrong and how to repair the damage. She determines to make him smile, to get his attention, to bring him back from his isolation, so he will once again illuminate her life.

To keep the flow of his affection constant, she must accurately map the geography of her father's wishes for compliance. It is clear to her that to secure his love she must obey him and respect his authority; she must be careful not to jeopardize her precarious position of his Princess by attitudes or behavior he disapproves of. Her own survival depends on knowing the limits of his tolerance.

Through trial and error, the clever daughter learns how to handle her father, secure his good will, and avoid his wrath. She conforms to his desire for a good daughter, a feminine daughter, by charting his limits and his prejudices. Her desire to please him is mixed with her longing to be special and her fear of rejection. If she goes too far, his disappointment may turn to rage and he will enforce his right to punish her. Afraid Dad will stop loving her, the daughter begins to present a more and more suppressed self, knowing that conformity to his wishes is her only real protection.

She gauges his threshold for acts of autonomy by watching his reactions, however subtle and seemingly inconsequential: a raised eyebrow, a scowl, a silence, a fist tightened and released, a muscle quivering in his cheek. She drops certain topics from her conversational repertoire, never referring to people, events, or ideas that he strongly opposes. Now and then she tests the waters to see if it is safe to broach her own thoughts, her own opinions, even if he may disagree with her. But the tension it creates seems to make her project self-defeating. Her mother silently implores her to give in, to apologize, to let her father win.

She protests that she wasn't contradicting him, or trying to make a fool of him, but feels unable to express her motives in a way he can understand and accept. She wants to disagree, to have the room to disagree, but she holds her tongue and remains silent. She has learned that he can regulate her speech, determining when it is appropriate and acceptable and when her silence is required. She learns that it is often easier to lie to him, to hide the truth about who she is and what she does, than to prove she has the right to make her own decisions and hold her own opinions. In any contest with her father, the daughter learns that unless she loses gracefully, she threatens their bond.

Yet, the privileges of speech and opinion are promised to

her as part of his benevolence, and he often reminds her that he is interested in her opinions, that he wants her to stand up for herself, that she often has good ideas. His appeal to her as a collaborator in discussion is seductive enough to allow the daughter to believe that he sincerely wishes her to speak her mind. He disclaims any resemblance to traditional authoritarian fathers, old-time patriarchs who rule with iron gloves, demanding obedience and compromise in order to be happy. He assures her that he is more modern, less rigid—a loving and protective man. But he never fails to impress upon his daughter that in the final analysis, he is the Father and his word, at least as long as she lives in *his* house, under *his* roof, eating the food that *he* puts on the table, is Law. She is obliged to recognize his authority and respect it, or else he will show her who is really the boss.

There comes a time when the beloved daughter, who has tried so hard to be herself and still be Daddy's Girl, feels betrayed by his pronouncements. How dare he demote her this way and treat her like any other of his subjects? He has told her that she was his special little girl, that she has a way with him, that he would try to give her what she wants, to make his girl as happy as he could. Now when he doesn't like the way she speaks to him he tells her she is taking too many liberties, that she had better watch her mouth. He warns her not to forget her place, reminding her that it is only by *his* good graces that she is allowed to get away with murder. As the daughter listens to this man, her father, telling her that only by conforming to his rules will she be assured of his affection, she realizes that if she doesn't want to lose him, she will have to submit.

In combat with the father the young daughter comes to understand what men require of "their" women. They seem to expect her to be willing to be seduced, betrayed, and seduced again. Because of his position in the world and in the family, the father does not consider any one act of obedience sufficient to remind the daughter that she is powerless before his authority. To get back in his good graces she has to forget the humiliation of losing to him, of feeling like a fool and helpless. As he jokes with her and tries to put their relationship back on a "normal" course, he assures her he is no longer angry, that he was just having fun, but of course she knows he is dead serious about winning.

She wants to stay angry at him, to punish him for using his place to ridicule her ideas and undermine her confidence in her opinions. She silently rages at him for stating the obvious—that she is under his control and, in effect, his whim. But her anger is short-lived because again and again he returns with promises of love. She wants to hate him but forgives him at the same time, since the thought of losing him seems unbearable. She tells him she is sorry, that she didn't mean to get him so angry, wouldn't ever purposely upset him. She assures him of her loyalty and promises to be good again.

In return for her self-denial and obedience the daughter is promised protection and support. In this way the father seeks to demonstrate to his daughter the proper attitudes that men and women should show toward each other. Depicting the world as somewhat overwhelming for his daughter, who seems rebellious enough to get into trouble but too timid to be able to handle it, he wants her to know that if she needs his help he will be there for her. "There are some things that your mother doesn't know much about, some things that men are better equipped to handle, so whenever you need my help, just ask."

Many times a daughter must turn to her father, asking for his advice, his opinion, or money. His willingness to spend money on the daughter is seen, by her and her mother, as a sure sign of the state of his affection. If he provides her with school fees or gives her money for clothes or after-school activities the daughter feels that he approves of her wants. But when he turns his daughter's requests for money into an opportunity to exchange compliance for control, the daughter recognizes the importance of using all her feminine skills to get what she needs. There is, of course, no guarantee of success, but since she knows what pleases him she is willing to appeal to him and his sense of duty, through her femininity. The daughter flatters her father, telling him that without his help she would not be able to do what is important to her. Stressing that she needs not only his good wishes but his money to keep up with the other girls, she hopes by shaming him to get her way. After all, she argues, he knows that she can't make it on her own, without his help. Look how often she has made him proud of her. Why can't he see that she needs him now?

The father wants his daughter to be like other girls, to have the possessions and skills that will make her fit in and succeed. As long as she acts right, and doesn't cause any trouble, he considers rethinking her demands. But she must be good. He likes her best when she acts as though she needs him, so when she lets him play the masculine to her feminine role, he comes through for her. He assures his daughter that if she appeals to other men the way she appeals to him, she will be a great success as a woman.

Whether she understands him or not, the daughter has become aware that her father's requirements for being his little girl include overt ritual bows to his authority, demonstrations of her acceptance of feminine subordination, and dependence on men. The daughter's reward for suppressing her willfulness and independence is her father's approval and promises of protection. The domain for protection is vast and the daughter sees herself as vulnerable in so many ways. Because her father represents the public world and indeed spends most of his life there, the daughter often accepts his world view and shares his fears about her inability to protect herself from the many exploitations to which the naive and innocent are inevitably subjected. If he has taken her side in conflicts at home with her mother, if he has strained to protect her from even his own anger, she feels he will always be there for her when she needs him and she is grateful. Idealizing his rigidity as strength, calling his acts of selfishness pride, seeing his petty tyrannies as attempts to keep her safe from danger, the daughter pays homage to the "superiority" of masculinity and feels safer when she has a secure connection to men, the more valuable and valued of the two gender groups. When she can share his view of the reciprocal obligations between men and women, paternal authority seems less chafing and his demands for compliance less oppressive.

The requirements for being good shift radically as the daughter approaches adolescence. "Being good," which has meant acting feminine, avoiding attitudes or behavior that did not fit the cultural stereotype for appropriate gender identity, extends in adolescence to the daughter's relationship to her sexuality. While the father has encouraged his daughter's heterosexual hopes by admiring her and rewarding the ways in which she conforms to femininity's mold, he has been careful to allow her some autonomy, perhaps because her independent streak reminded him of himself and the ways she was "his" daughter too. Yet to encourage self-directed action when she is going to confront sexual demands may be dangerous. For her own good Dad now extends his authority over her activities with her male peers. He claims his paternal duties and obligations which include protecting her sexual purity.

As the daughter begins to look more like a woman than a child, new tension is added to the father-daughter relationship. Her father is shut out of many conversations, since they revolve around the world of exclusively feminine concerns: being popular, looking pretty, having boyfriends. The daughter has a strong desire to lead her own life, which means she will have to close her parents out of some areas of her activities and thoughts. The daughter wants more privacy, to spend more time away from home, and more privileges than have previously been accorded her. Entering adolescence, she wants to shed her childish ways yet be assured of not losing the love and affection of the people she cares about most.

The daughter wants her father to confirm her potential success in this new arena and to approve of her becoming a woman and an adult. She wants him to appreciate that the new changes will not alter their relationship and that she will not leave him behind. She tries to reassure him that she doesn't require the tight surveillance he wants to set up for her, that he needn't worry about her safety because she can really take care of herself. Even if she can't fully convince herself that leaving home is free from danger, she tries to convince her father that she will always be his little girl and loyal to him.

To reassure him and herself that she will succeed as a heterosexual woman, the daughter solicits compliments from her father for her fledgling attempts at becoming an object of appeal. She absorbs his comments about the qualities he finds attractive in women and tries to adopt those traits. She notices his attention to women on the street and on television, and listens to his remarks about those he considers cheap and those who are "real dishes." She knows that he, of all people, should be able to tell her whether she looks unfeminine or dresses or acts in a way that would turn boys off. She mentally records his criticism, notes his idiosyncratic tastes, stands before him nervously awaiting his judgment, and hopes to win an appreciative smile. She places her femininity on the line for his approval because his opinion, as a man's, counts more than her mother's.

If Dad pays attention to his daughter's transformation and responds with pleasure to her desire for heterosexual affirmation, the daughter feels she has been given a wonderful gift. If he notices her newly sexualized femininity, she feels her existence has been illuminated. If he is indifferent or resentful of these changes and refuses to acknowledge the tension they have created between them, she may think her desires to be grown up are wrong and hurt her father. In some psychologically important way, the daughter needs her father's approval to feel she can leave him.

She knows it is within Dad's rights, as he and Mom have defined them, to control her access to the world outside the family, to monitor her activities for hints of wrongdoing and to impose restrictions and prohibitions on the company she keeps. A sentry, a judge, and a jury. Just as he acts as arbiter of her place and fate in the family, he plays that role as she seeks autonomy in the world. The daughter may question his privileges and rebel against the severity of the new rules for her conduct, but she knows she cannot openly challenge his control over her actions and her body. As long as she lives in *his* house, she has to operate according to his rules or maneuver around them. The latter, more dangerous, route can cause the real tension between them to explode and leave the daughter facing the fact of her father's sexual jealousy which she both likes and fears.

Partly to protect Dad from the reality of her moving away

from him, and partly because she wants to preserve her good feelings about exploring the world without him, the daughter resorts to keeping secret her interest in sexual experimentation. She thinks it better to maintain her assigned feminine position of sexual indifference. She knows that her goodness protects her from accusations of badness, and when badness stands for sexuality, the pressure to act circumspectly is increased. The daughter doesn't want her father to think she is bad, but neither does she want to forego testing her sexual attractiveness with her peers. Yet the only way to hold him is to give up her self—or have sex behind his back.

Sometimes she enlists her mother to cover for her, even for her most "innocent" meetings with boys. Both women want to protect Father and themselves. A man, the daughter learns, cannot bear the knowledge that access to "his women" is not under "his control." He must somehow be convinced that the daughter accepts his surveillance as an act of love rather than suppression. Possessive and jealous of her potential to give herself to other men, the father withdraws his affection. There are long periods of coldness and poorly disguised disgust. He threatens physical punishment, perhaps for the first time, to show the daughter that he means business. Her sexual purity is his Holy Grail, and he will protect her from social sanctions and his own fury only if he can be assured of her goodness—her sexual purity. Living in Dad's house, Daughter learns that real or feigned sexual abstinence will be necessary to maintain her father's respect, approval, and love.

This unstated but comprehended request for sexual self-repression and denial leaves the daughter to choose between pleasing her father and pleasing herself. The choice is sometimes made more difficult because the threat of physical punishment is mixed with the threat of loss of love. The daughter may want to believe that her father wants to protect her for her own good, that he is thinking only of teenage pregnancy, a bad reputation, or the unspoken and unspeakable dangers of an early loss of "innocence." She doesn't want to "cheat on him," but she doesn't want to be bullied by his sexual jealousy. The daughter can remain a virgin until she leaves her father's house, or she can hide her "bad" activities and continue to be his little girl.

Whatever the daughter decides to do in this situation, she cannot predict what her father's jealousy will produce. No matter whether she is "good"—asexual—or "bad"—sexual—she must live with his suspicions and restrictions to keep from provoking him and losing his love. Despite the flush of power she feels as she begins to attract men's attentions, she knows her powers are no match for his. She tries to be careful, not wearing too much makeup, a skirt that is too revealing, a blouse that shows the outlines of her breasts. By toning herself down, she hopes to keep his attention and not provoke his disapproval.

But her father waits up for her return from a date, sitting there looking at the clock, ready to interrogate her about her activities. If his masculinity is truly threatened he implies she has no judgment about men, that is, boys, that she is just a poor babe in the woods. He tells her that men only want to "take advantage" of her and she must not allow that to happen. He says he could never respect her if she didn't respect herself, adding that boys feel the same way about girls. Her father isn't interested in her explanations about how she was just sitting in the car talking; he isn't a fool. He knows how young men's minds work—after all, he was once young himself—and she is a pretty girl, so he understands that boys will want to use her.

The daughter is shocked when Dad doesn't trust her anymore and confused about his fear of her becoming bad, or, in fact, already being bad. Does he know something about her that she can't yet see? Is there something inside her that will lead to her being called unladylike, unfeminine? She has never heard him talk this way before and is stunned that he can be set off so easily by anything she does that points to her desires for sexual and social autonomy.

Sometimes the father cannot contain his reactions to losing his daughter and his control over her sexual autonomy. If he catches her trying on a vampish look in the bathroom mirror or petting with her boyfriend, or finds she has obtained birth control pills and is having sex, he suddenly reaches his limit and explodes, with curses and fists flying. He calls her a whore, a tramp, a no-good cock-teaser, a slut, a nympho, and a fool. Frustrated or enraged, the father curses the woman in her, her sexual aspect, which becomes the hallmark of her femininity in the world and in his eyes. He may raise his hands to her, slam her against the wall, pound her head against the floor, beating her into goodness. Her mother stands by, wringing her hands and whimpering for him to stop; Mother and Daughter plead for him to stay his blows, to consider how sorry he will feel if he should hurt his own child; they beg him to show mercy.

Slapped, punched, kicked, and cursed at, Daddy's Girl wonders if her father is right in thinking her no better than a whore, but then realizes this gross exaggeration. She was only pursuing her own pleasure. Does she have to beg his forgiveness for that too? Stunned by the force of his reaction she stares in wonder as the man she has known in his many incarnations of rationality, even compulsive reason, turns into a wild and raging beast. Does this sign of fury mean that he no longer loves her or just that he loves her too much? Men are so difficult to understand.

The daughter's sense of being special to her father, transformed by her threatened leave-taking, is amplified and assured in adolescence. It both infuriates and gratifies the daughter to find him so obsessed with her possible sexual activities and know that he always has his eye on her. Even her father's denunciations and blows seem to reveal his passion for her and her success as a "woman." She is aware of new ways to get his attention, and being thought bad is just as effective as being thought good. Maybe even better. She knows she can hurt or please him by her choices in expressing or repressing her sexuality.

The Daddy's Girl learns a crucial lesson, one not easily forgotten in all later love relations. To find her father's favor she has to lose herself, curb her desires for autonomous action, and renounce in the name of love her longings for independence. She is reminded that men's attention feels good, and her father's attention, even expressed negatively, makes her feel alive and worthy. She may not want to confront the necessity of choosing to please either men or herself, but she is familiar with that dilemma. Sexual fidelity, first to her father, then to her lover, male or female, assures that the daughter is safe and loved. But sexual repression in the name of love and being feminine is a powerful call to sexual self-denial that is difficult to silence. A daughter who wants to keep the love of her first heterosexual love has to abide by the rules of gender and renounce unfeminine desires for sexual gratification through autonomous sexual choice. If she expects one day to find a man, and have her sexual wishes granted, she has to devote some of her energies to sexual self-repression, so that she will appear desirable, and thus feminine, to the world. Unfeminine women who pursue their own pleasure do not deserve men's protection. The desiring woman is unfeminine.

The father-daughter relationship is the laboratory for learning heterosexuality, in its sexual and social aspects; it prepares the daughter to enter the world with an accurate map of the heterosexual status quo. First, in observing her parents' behavior with each other, she acknowledges her father's treatment as a man and her mother's as a woman. She concludes that men love to rule and women to serve. Or do they perhaps express their love for each other in these gender-specific ways? She learns her mother's fear that not pleasing him and protecting him from criticism, even her own, could result in his walking out, leaving her without someone to love her. The daughter doesn't want to provoke him into leaving; her mother would never forgive her if she did. So she and Mother try to be good for him, to show him that he is special and must be kept happy.

Through her identification with her mother the daughter knows that when she loves a man, as her mother does her father, she will have to act the same way. Unless she finds a man unlike her father. Or if she ends up being unlike her mother. But given the way society is organized the daughter cannot stray far from the mold for feminine heterosexuality. Her choices are overdetermined.

Daughter's intense relationship with Father, her need to please him, and the pleasure she feels when she makes him happy—or angry—when she can get his attention result in her desire to play that role again. He has helped her to understand the power of her demeanor as a proper sexual woman.

Daddy's Girl likes to be cared for, to have her choices made, her future decided because such treatment reinforces her schooling in the ways men show their love. Dad says he wants to do for her, to give her things, to be in control. And never sure of her father's willingness to confirm her femininity, she seeks a man who will speak and act more openly.

No matter how she rails against him, refuses his influence, and fights his authority, the Princess will always find it difficult to accuse her father of having been unloving, even if he was unjust. His conservatism is a source of security and his authority still looms large in her head. The irony for Daddy's Girls is that they are in love not only with the man, but his authority and power.

Through idealizing her father, a daughter can advance her romance with men with little obstruction. Despite or because of punishments and taunts mixed with love and praise, the daughter turns to men to gain their acceptance, to see if she has the womanly traits they like. Because she wanted to win her father but failed, she determines to try again. Because the charge in their relationship came from the fusion of eroticism and extremes of power and inequality, she looks for that electricity again, turned on by the passive pleasure of giving up control. Because her attachment to her father is so old and her love for him so deep, she is often unaware that she seeks to create situations in which a man will take care of her.

If the bonds of love between her and her father were strong, the daughter may continue to believe her search for power is a betrayal of men and a threat to her own notion of feminine propriety. In deferring to her father she not only avoided his anger and discipline, but gained his praise. Her submission brought him pleasure; her pleasure was to make him happy. Forgetting his judgment flouted convention and the rules of safety. Acting in her own interests brought threats of withdrawal of the warmth of his love. Because the Princess has been cold for so long and hungry for the affection and esteem routinely denied to girls, she depends on her father, and later on other men, to make her feel like a real woman, like Daddy's Girl again.

From her father she learns her place, her privileges, her rewards, and her punishments. If she forgets her place in the heterosexual gender-play, she will have to answer to other male authorities and explain the meaning of her unfeminine behavior. But the Princess usually commits her allegiance to the man who helped her rehearse the role she must play and is prepared to defend.

Daddy's Girl pleases her father because she has learned the sure way to get men's attention and love. She is willing to put her energy into servicing a man, understanding him, and anticipating his demands, because she feels better about herself when she knows she has the power to make him love her. Daddy's power, his very real acts of sadism and cruelty, and his softness and vulnerability are attractive and the consequences of loving the powerful from a position of powerlessness are eroticized, as the daughter is bound by love to the first man who personifies masculinity and its privileges.

4
THE FAMILY ROMANCE

Each parent encourages a different aspect of femininity in the daughter. Mom wants her good and helpful, Dad wants her pretty and helpless. Instead of cancelling each other out, however, the contradictions of femininity are exacerbated by the dynamics of the nuclear family.

I

The family is a place of great scarcity. The nuclear family is supposed to be a haven from the hostile, alien world, a nest for sheltering children until they are armed and ready to venture out, a sanctuary for the tired warrior, and an oasis of warmth, peace, and love. But the nuclear family consists of a tiny band of inadequately prepared, ill-equipped adults who have been taught as men and women to fear and despise each other, thrust into a material situation that militates against their ever developing a warm, friendly, supportive set of relationships. In addition, the adults in the family are inundated with propaganda about how they *should* feel that is totally unrelated to the realities they face. This, at the very least, confuses them, and they are forced to reproduce their neuroses in their children because they don't realize that they need outside help, don't feel entitled to it, don't know how to get it, and have been taught to distrust it. So they don't demand help, and as a result there is none to be had. The family, terribly anemic and vastly overburdened, is not a good place for a child to grow up in.

In most nuclear families, Mom, Dad, and the kids relate to each other primarily on the basis of scarcity and competition rather than on surplus and cooperation because there simply isn't enough love, interest, and attention to go around. Mom cannot possibly work outside the home and take care of several growing, needy children, or stay home with several small, needy, growing children without going sour. Dad cannot possibly work enough to feed the family, and then come home to supply Mom with the adult, collegial companionship and stimulation she needs after a day with the children or overcome his masculine training and voluntarily relinquish his privileges to share equally in the family chores with Mom. Even a dad who wants to participate has to be taught, encouraged, fought with, urged, rewarded—hardly a fair burden on Mom, who has to do all that and her own share as well. The problem is that there is nobody else. The nuclear family is based on exclusion (scarcity). We are supposed to find mates and then do everything with each other, just each other, and if we can't we've failed.

We all fail, and we all learn to compete, to scramble for whatever time, attention, resources, and love there is. We may sometimes agree on who should come first, but if we don't receive some of our quota we can't give anyone else much. Even a shared appreciation of somebody else's greater momentary need is based on competition. Quantitative comparison is meaningful only in periods of scarcity. Life in the nuclear family is a constant struggle to get on the agenda—to gain attention, to bargain for one's right to various kinds of attention, and, simultaneously, to attempt to avoid the flack and shift the burden onto someone else. Our relationships to our parents are based largely on unfulfilled needs, to our siblings on endlessly betrayed alliances. There are also the eternally haunting questions about the relationships of others in the family: Which child do the parents prefer? If one is pretty and one is good, which is better? If one is so different from the other, how can Dad like both? What do they see in each other? What do they see in us?

Most families, let's say, follow a similar pattern of child treatment. The older ones are allowed to do a little more and the boys have it a little better, but nobody is clearly the favorite, nobody clearly the outcast. In the family hierarchy, kids are much closer to each other than they are to their parents. What the parents have, over and above everyone else in the family (in addition to control over the economic resources), is an exclusive sexual bond. Whatever else happens, as much as they may turn to any one of the children, they get into bed together at night. Even if they sleep in separate beds, they have slept together before and might again. They may give children love, attention, and devotion, but they give sex only to each other.

The exclusiveness of the parents' sexual bond is the central piece of the nuclear family and determines what happens in the family. Because emotional resources are scarce, and sex is a complex emotional exchange (or is supposed to be, as opposed to a "purely physical" exchange, which is considered inferior in our culture), it is bound to appear like a rather large chunk of the available nourishment. No matter what parents tell them about sex children see the mother-father relationship, which determines much of their universe, as profoundly connected with sex in some way they can only try to figure out. It looms large even if they never think about it directly.

Very young children know only that they want and need Mom. She is their life-support system. At some point, usually around the second year of life, they become aware of Mom's attention to Dad (or someone in his role). They need her badly because they haven't been getting as much of her as they might and are starved for her. Children feel this need acutely as they try to venture out, to separate, to make their way from her side into the world. By the time they can walk and start to communicate in sentences, they are poised for intellectual, physical, and emotional exploration, and have to be sure that the life-support system is firmly in place. (The space walk is a piece of cake compared to this.) They notice that Mom gives Dad all the attention they want. Frequently, it seems, when they risk going a few steps from her side, she's not there when they turn back because she is busy with him. They feel envy, jealousy, and rage. They want what he's getting; they want him to stop getting it, and they want her to stop giving it to him and give it to them. They feel rejected by Mom because she does not give them what they want and jealous of Dad because she gives it to him. They want him out of the picture. They reject him. If they could, they'd push the button and eject him right out of the family, leaving just Mom and them—like it used to be.

But Dad, in the normal course of affairs, does not just die because children want him to. He stays. (They have a worse time if he actually goes: Their anger has made him disappear; they are mighty but evil!) He keeps taking pieces of Mom whenever he feels like it. That secret, special bond they have keeps holding. Their anger shifts from Dad, the intruder, to Mom, the betrayer. She really *is* choosing him! With her choice she keeps rejecting them. Mom will not get rid of Dad, he's there to stay, and he has a lot of power. He can get her whenever he wants, for instance, and he can tell them what to do. And they need someone to fill the gap, starved as they are. So they consider Dad and turn to him. They need someone and, mad at Mom, they want to punish her for rejecting them. So forget her! They turn to Dad who they discover is not of much use either: He has an exclusive sexual bond with her! Now they want him, want to be powerful like him, be protected by him, nurtured by him. And he keeps handing them back to her, keeps having sex with her! They feel jealous of her, furious at her. Now they wish to eject Mom from the family so they can take her place with Dad.

But she usually stays. Anger can't kill her either. The failure hurts. Children are forced to deal with the incontrovertible fact that Mom and Dad have an exclusive relationship, and that they are outsiders. Their tremendous anger at both their parents helps them move away from home base a little, to venture farther into the world outside themselves. It is development fuel. At the same time, children still need Mom and Dad desperately: They can't yet survive on their own. Parents supply all children's needs, on every conceivable level, so children can't afford to focus too much time on anger at parents. Anger provokes Mom and Dad to punishment. Children channel their anger into constructive activities, turning to other sources: falling in love with a first-grade teacher, learning to supplement the family gruel with outside nourishment, to delay gratification and pine for lost objects, to fall in love with unattainable people. They prepare to wait it out. Puberty will be a trial, but if they get through that all right, they'll grow up and marry someone just like Mom or Dad—which is only second best to marrying Mom or Dad, of course. But children who weren't disillusioned in the family long before learn in school and on the playground that you can't marry your parents.

They turn to their peers and siblings, who are in the same position they are—not getting enough either. They can band together, allies for a time, but can't really supply each other's needs, so the alliance is doomed. Children need the grown-ups and have to learn to compete for them.

Childhood friendships are fraught with envy, jealousy, and juggling for position. The only saving grace is that everybody plays by the rules. There is a hierarchy in which one's place can be determined; one can have equals (on one's level in the hierarchy), which is evident to anyone who knows her or his way around the schoolyard. And there are ways to move up and down the ladder in a predictable fashion. It is not unlike the family hierarchy at home, but much more open and easier to understand. Mom and Dad start to recede into the background of childish fantasies. Children become much more preoccupied with their personal lives than with family matters.

Children whose early environment is relatively nourishing, rich in resources, attention, warmth, and encouragement, as well as affection, have a reasonably good chance of growing into strong, healthy, independent people, even with the original handicap of the nuclear family. But most do not grow up in an environment particularly suited to the developmental needs of children and adolescents. Most grow up in spite of the obstacles carefully put in their way by society's customs and institutions, in families that do not encourage trust in outsiders, even when it is warranted.

Parents usually have plenty of reason to mistrust the world and tend to teach that the boundaries of trust lie in bloodlines (or marriage contracts), which is a terribly misleading notion. People inside families often hurt their kin more than outsiders do (incest, child abuse, battering, neglect, deprivation, sheer ignorance), and outsiders sometimes offer genuine help. People outside the family can save the lives of those whose families are closing in on or throwing them out.

So the criteria for trusting people become mysterious. Children learn that they have to find that one person, that Mr. (or Ms) Right who, by virtue of becoming one of the family will be considered trustworthy. But with the exception of the marriage hunt, they are rarely encouraged to find real nourishment and companionship outside the family. Unless they connect with someone the family can adopt, they are made to feel they are engaging in an illicit relationship.

The myths about the nuclear family prevent children from seeking appropriate alternatives to the exclusive, provocative relationship between their parents, or to the rivalries with their siblings. Boys and girls are told they must love their families, whose members can and will gratify all their needs. They feel disloyal when they enjoy being with outsiders who can help them. So children stay tied up in the family, trying to squeeze enough out of it, trying to subsist on and fighting for every available scrap. They resolve the conflict between their anger at and need for parents by repressing it, by closing their eyes, swallowing bad feelings, and trying again. They try to compete with each one of their parents for the other, caught up in the family romance.

II

As daughters, we stay caught up in the romance of the family because we need our parents in different ways. We need Mom. We need *a* mom, that is, a source of comfort and warmth and safety. Someone who makes it better when life gets rough, who can ultimately clear up mix-ups and misunderstandings, who will not let us sulk too long after a fight, who will guide us back into the game. Someone who will validate and accept us, regardless. As daughters, we require mothers who have faith in us, hope for us, whose concern is boundless and steady, because life gets rockier, more dangerous, and we are expected to handle more of it ourselves. Mom must be there to welcome us back from our adventures, beaming, ready and able to somehow turn the worst disaster into a positive, worthwhile, learning experience. Mom must reassure us that we will be the better for it, that everything is really all right.

But few moms are like that. Each mother is the best approximation of the ideal she can carry off, and the odds are all against her. Mothers feel tired, incompetent, harassed, frustrated, lonely, sick, and are often in despair. We may trigger some of these feelings, and although many are unrelated to us, Mom may vent her feelings on us or withhold her love and benign attention inappropriately. Timing is a big problem. We may bask in Mom's good moods but know better than to trust them because experience tells us these feelings won't last, might not be there the next time they're needed. We don't entirely understand the causes of the bad moods and try to shoulder whatever blame Mom assigns. The blame feeds our neglected egos negatively, and we try to attribute some of it to the rest of the family—siblings and Dad. We experience Mom's bad moods as a rejection of us.

As daughters, we also feel jealous. We see Mom looking at Dad, and sometimes at our siblings, the way we want to be looked at, with a special glance. We feel that Mom prefers them, that she really loves Dad, whether she lets on or not. Dad influences her moods more than anyone, or seems to. We know that Mom is "in love" with Dad (or was, or could be, or might be), and, no matter how much she loves us, won't ever be in love with us. And Dad won't be in love with us either, not the way he is with Mom. We need his attention too. Everything in the house underscores the fact that he is the most important person. His feelings determine the rhythm of the household. His face causes the sun to rise or set. What happens, happens when he comes home. Our home is *his* castle.

Dad bestows worth and assigns merit. To be chosen by him means to be special. As daughters, we learn to look forward to being chosen by him as life's goal: to get a man to love and marry us. Dad is the source of power, the fountainhead, and we want to cuddle close, to feel that power envelop and save us from harm. Dad is the ultimate authority, the savior we need close by. But he keeps rejecting us for Mom. He is nice to us

up to a point, but then he goes to bed with Mom. He wants
something from Mom that we identify with and want too, but
he gets it, or so we suspect. Then there is the way Dad wants
Mom: all that exuberance, that wildness and joy we feel when
Dad lifts us up in his strong arms—Mom gets that too. Mom
somehow gets to go on, to be lifted in his arms endlessly, to
take off. We don't quite know what it is or how it happens, but
we envy it and are jealous. It's not fair! We need them both in
different ways, Mom for life and Dad for everything else, yet
they constantly reject us for each other. We are torn with jealousy for both of them, excluded from both, trapped with both.
We have no choice but to keep trying to win one of them.

As daughters, we have to strive for the impossible unless we
learn to take what we can use from what is available and get
it anywhere we can. Most parents don't offer conscious, gentle
weaning because they need *us*. So we end up stuck in a triangular nightmare, endlessly repeated. We feel, about both our parents, a terrible mixture of desperate need, desolate rejection,
burning jealousy, and choking rage. And we want our parents
to adore us exclusively, so that anything short of total adoration
is further proof that they don't love us. They are too busy getting involved with each other. Our only hope is to break it up,
to find a way to turn the camera around and onto us. We have
to find a way to break the alliance, to get each parent to resolve
the stalemate by spontaneously turning to us. No more tension,
no more tears! We try to get to each parent individually, to play
each off against the other. We choose between the parents endlessly, fantasizing divorce, what we'd say when the judge asks us
which parent we want to live with. It's like an Academy Award
acceptance speech: We get to say our piece, to do the dedication, to include and exclude after eloquently summing up their
good and bad points, to wield the power.

If parents assure that we lose the campaign unequivocally
(though never absolutely), we may learn to give up and find a
more satisfying alternative elsewhere. Rather than remaining
fixed on the painful picture of sparks flying between them, we
generate some sparks of our own, with someone willing to play

with *us*. But most parents defeat us very ambiguously, ambivalently, inconsistently. One minute they're telling us to get going, get out, and the next minute to watch out, be careful. How can one get going while being careful? If one were being careful, one wouldn't go! Parents say, "Leave us alone, but don't ever leave us. Don't come crying to us, but don't go around crying to strangers. Figure it out for yourself, but come up with the answer we expect."

So, as daughters, we keep trying to figure it out, to get a clue to parents' coded conversations. We strive to read the message written in the sparks that zip back and forth between Mom and Dad and in the fallout that comes our way. We are mesmerized, hooked, standing in front of the jump rope, waiting to jump in, trying to get the rhythm. But parents keep changing the beat somehow, and we can't figure out how they're doing it in unison. If we could see and learn to read the signals between them, we could anticipate the new rhythm and join Mom and Dad. But we keep missing it, and every time we jump in, it's wrong, and even when we're in, jumping well, we can't relax for a minute because the rhythm could change again. We have to keep outguessing the rope. It feels like torture: Monkey in the middle, and we're exhausted, and we can't catch the ball, and we can't afford to drop out. But at least we're in the middle. It's worse when we're outside, still trying to find the right moment to jump in, which never comes. We spend a lot of time watching the rope's rhythm. The worst times come when we watch others jump in smoothly and take over. Suddenly, it looks as though the rope swingers are merely there to facilitate the performance of the jumpers. The spotlight is on the new jumper. She is just gliding in and out and around the rope and the two on either end are totally focused on her, and all three of them make up one gorgeous, graceful dance, and they look exhilarated and joyful.

So we get hooked, addicted to jumping rope. We need to get in there and jump; it kills us to watch from the outside, it eats us up. When our turn finally comes, the turners ask us in, we're paralyzed with fear, stuck in a nightmare. Then, when we dare the unthinkable and jump in, we either have to face the ultimate humiliation—tripping over the rope and making complete asses of ourselves—or start jumping and become stuck. There is no way out; we have to keep jumping, even when our sides hurt and we're out of breath and our feet are killing us; there is no way to stop the game, no way to resolve it. As long as parents keep swinging the rope, we have to keep jumping. We feel like puppets, but whenever they swing the rope, we have to jump in. We wait to be asked to join in, we get ourselves to jump toward the swinging rope, and then we have to keep jumping. It becomes a way of life we set up ourselves. We find a partner for anyone we care about, then hand them a rope and urge them to start swinging it. We then feel at home, in a panic, in a familiar kind of pain. If only we could break out and relate to people one at a time. But we can't. We keep triangulating, finding our way back into that familiar painful situation we grew up in, dangling from that rope between Mom and Dad.

The differences between us evolve from our available solutions to this addiction. Depending on the particular nature of our family situation, the power differential between parents, for example, or the supplies available in the family's emotional economy—the acuteness of unfulfilled needs, the extent of deprivation—we handle the family romance differently. There are styles of jumping rope. We each do it in a unique way, but within recognizable categories. One way to describe it is to focus on the different approaches to the triangle dilemma resulting from training to be more a Good Girl or more a Princess. Given the cultural environment that insists girls have to become feminine, the choice of prescribed responses is limited. The emergence of the Good Girl (Mommy's Girl) part of us or the Princess (Daddy's Girl) part of us is a reflection of the parent who is more ambiguous in weaning or rejecting us.

III

The Good Girl in us hopes to get Mom in the end. She needs Mom and Mom needs her to soothe away the ache of her deprivation. Mom gets her message across with compliments or supposedly innocuous comments. Mommy's Girl strikes a bargain: "I'll be what you want me to be, whatever you need, if you'll just love me and take care of me." Mom agrees. Her girl is her comfort, the friend she can't do without. Mommy's Girl is mature for her age, and that's good because she's more useful that way. Mom would be in trouble without her girl, who fills the void left by Dad's supposedly unsatisfactory attentions. Mom's message is mysterious but it gives us hope: The Good Girl could become more important to Mom than anyone else, including Dad. Mommy's Girl is thrilled that she might win and be Mom's favorite person. She doesn't know how or what or why and has only vague ideas and felt signals that are hard to decipher, but it's enough to hook her. She stays plugged into the family triangle, playing for Mom.

Mom wants her daughter to be "sensitive." Sensitive is a complex mixture of contradictory elements when used to describe feminine "nature." It means, for one thing, that a woman has to approach everything on an emotional basis. Intellectual curiosity, pragmatic concerns, or philosophical analysis should come, if ever, only after she has navigated the onslaught of her swirling or fluttering feelings. When an unfortunate incident occurs, for instance, she's supposed to feel sad. If she doesn't really feel sad, but curious instead, she's supposed to feel guilty. If she doesn't feel guilty, she's supposed to feel bad about herself, disapproving, because she's so insensitive. As she walks through the world with her feelings foremost, she has to make sure her feelings don't hinder feminine compliance. She is taught to follow, to fit in, to adapt. So her responses always have to be carefully modulated, never take over or take off. Everything has to be muted. Tantrums of any kind upset Mom. She learns that it's not right to demand attention. She has to deserve attention, to barter for it while watching Mom vigilantly for any change in her feelings, never letting her eyes wander off her for a minute, always ready to respond in an emotional way.

If she's too emotional and not compliant enough, she's called hysterical and accused of selfishly seeking attention. If not emotional enough, she runs the risk of being called "cold and analytic" (just like her father). Rational approaches to events are not feminine. A really good girl has to find the perfect middle road: sensitive, empathic, understanding, always ready to help and comfort, never preoccupied with her own reactions or concerns, though regularly overwhelmed by them (when nobody else needs her). The Good Girl is always on call, ready to serve.

Mommy's Girl has to learn to walk a fine line to please Mom, to become sensitive and compliant and still manage to grow up. Mom has little use for a baby she has to care for and attend to constantly. She needs a friend, a confidante, someone who will understand her, care about her, and make it all up to her. Her daughter realizes increasingly that she owes Mom her life, that Mom is trying to raise her right and doesn't have it easy either. Mommy's Girl feels she should be living a life that will make it up to Mom, wants to live for her, and would never intentionally do anything to hurt or abandon her. She learns, in short, to turn it all around: to grow up into Mommy's Little Mother.

The Good Girl gives up pieces of her childhood and much of her right to become the person she dreams of. She grows up because Mom needs her that way. Growing up means mastery, independence, the ability to negotiate the world. She dedicates these skills to Mom (and "the family"), without whom, she honestly believes, none of her achievements would have been possible. She learns to use those skills on Mom's behalf rather than on her own. She doesn't want to be selfish because Mom disapproves. So she learns to be pleased by helping people rather than by getting others to do what she wants (that would be "manipulative"). She learns to take responsibility only for actions that go wrong, not those that work out. Mom disapproves of bragging.

And yet, she has to be clever, be a good girl. She has to know how to make things happen, how to figure out what others might want. She can't help others if she acts too dumb. She has to try to understand adult matters, to give comfort when grownups are needy and she can't really understand what the problem is because adults just hint but never really explain. She has to learn to say the "right" thing in all sorts of situations, including times when she's going to get in trouble with other kids for what she does and says. Kids are not enamored of mature goody-goody types. They make fun of and see through girls who just want to make points with Mom, who don't have pure motives. Kids know how cutthroat the competition is and that all of them are trying to win.

But Mom can't know. If she catches on she accuses her daughter of being calculating. So a good daughter has to find ways of sounding sincere. That takes a good deal of courage and cleverness. Often she fails. She says something "right" and "mature," but Mom lets her know she doesn't believe it, and that she sees her for the phony she really is. It's humiliating, but it's also confusing: The daughter usually has no idea what makes the difference between the times she does it and Mom loves it, eats it up, calls her astute, and the times when Mom doesn't buy it. The daughter thinks she's doing the same thing each time. Mom says the difference lies in whether or not her girl "means it." Her girl learns to mean it, to become genuinely filled with concern for Mom, world peace, and those less fortunate than herself so that none of that phony selfishness remains visible. That requires cleverness too.

A good daughter has to become competent. She must respond to the world primarily with feelings, with sensitivity, empathy, and concern. And she must learn how to make the world better. She must learn how to heal and give succor and nourish along and sustain and support, but must never recognize her power. Changing the environment is an option given to women only in modest, restricted doses. Women can change things a little for the better, but never claim our achievements. We are allowed to think of our impact on the world as that of a mother, a nurturer, an obedient worker in someone else's vineyard who keeps tending the vines, but who would be absurd (and immoral) if she were suddenly to decide she is making those vines grow, that they are her production.

So we must hide our competence by combining it with amiable, feminine vagueness. Clear, noticeable competence looks cold and hard on a woman. People tend to assume that such a woman is very competitive, very ruthless, and very selfish. If a Good Girl hides her competence, if she dithers before and after so that everyone can see it doesn't come easy even though it keeps coming, then it's all right. Other women won't hate her. If she gets upset about a small detail a man wouldn't even be expected to notice (and certainly not get all flustered over), she doesn't seem quite so coldly competent, and she certainly dispels any suspicion that she is proud of herself. That way, if she does a job in a vague but reliable way, without calling undue attention to her competence, she is being a good girl, cooperative. She can help others, be useful to them, but the others are always at least equal partners in the transaction when it comes to taking credit. She makes her modest contribution to someone else's endeavor but doesn't appropriate it. She is a helpmeet, a good sport, a great asset, never the genius. The Good Girl is very useful that way, willing to do practically anything for anybody, and she can, too. But she does it without threatening anyone's superiority.

If Mommy's Girl calls attention to her cleverness, Mom is not amused. She thinks it's selfish and petty to bask in glory or wallow in triumph. It makes other people feel bad. Mommy's Girl knows Mom is right, of course, because she feels bad to be continuously outdone by others and she joins her mother in the assumption that everyone would feel that way about her if she stood out in the crowd. Mommy's Girl is on her way to sainthood, she's better than most people—that's what she wants to be (saying that she thinks she is would be prideful so she keeps it to herself). She doesn't mind pain. She swallows her pride and lets others shine. All that swallowed pride and fear and pain and anger are going to come bubbling up somehow, of course, since she is no different from other humans even though she is a saint-in-training. The constant battle to suppress and berate her "bad" self is what keeps her humble and neurotic: There is always plenty of evidence that she's not as good as she should be. And any protestations from her loved ones (including Mom herself) that she's good only serve to pain her further: She's lying, appearing better than she really is. It makes her feel all the more anxious that one day she will be exposed for the terrible fraud she is. Sainthood is a terrible burden on a little girl, but irresistible when it offers the only way to walk into the sunset with Mom.

So the Good Girl grows up a failed saint, never giving up the hope that someday she will merge with Mom again. Meanwhile, back in the family romance, Mom is not the only player the daughter has to deal with. Dad often fails to make it clear that he really prefers Mom. His girl feels about him the way Mom does: He is the most important person in the house, when he's there. He is treated differently from the rest of the family. He is the prize. His daughter wants him. And he lets her know that Mom does not serve him adequately. She frequently gives him a hard time, as she does her children, and Dad and his daughter can sympathize with each other. Not necessarily out loud, of course, but there is enough evidence to believe that Dad has more in common with his girl, would be better off with someone like her, than with the woman he married. Mom just doesn't understand him, or doesn't like to have fun the way he does, or just doesn't appreciate him, or is not good enough for him. Daddy's Girl is going to be the kind of woman he wants/needs/likes/respects/should have married. She is like that already, in a way. And he appreciates the parts of his girl Mom is always down on.

True, Dad also wants his girl to be compliant and emotional, to feel deeply in prescribed ways, but he likes a bit of hysteria every now and then. Or rather he seems to enjoy when his girl acts in a way Mom considers overdone. He is more likely to melt when his girl lays it on, when she sobs uncontrollably and pitifully. He will even tolerate an emotional response that manifests itself in a rather loud, assertive way. He may not know how to respond to a crying daughter, but he certainly is affected in a way that leads her to recognize a weapon, one of those feminine ways she has to cultivate. She gets her way with him more when she's conspicuous. Mom may even teach her how to "get around" him. She learns to flirt professionally. He doesn't like it if she does it clumsily, if her intent is too overt; he likes a good game. She communicates in winks and nods, agreeing to their play acting. As long as they're clearly crazy about each other, clearly find each other irresistible, are surely ideally mated, he'll allow her to wrap him around her little finger because she's so cute. Mom and the Good Girl in us consider this kind of behavior phony, but it works, and it's also a lot of fun. It's exciting, risky, strenuous, and challenging.

Dad likes to challenge his daughter a little. He likes his Princess to be clever. Of course he doesn't necessarily want her to be a bluestocking or a genius, but he enjoys a good discussion or a little spunky teasing. He may agree with Mom that being too obviously smart can be a drawback for women because other men, later, won't be able to deal with cleverness, won't like it. But meanwhile, he doesn't see anything wrong with a little of it. He enjoys hearing his daughter make smart comments about people. Mom may think "smart-ass" is not a nice label to throw at a girl, but Dad kind of likes it. He doesn't mind if his girl is a little "catty"; he expects it. If not carried too far, it's natural in women, kind of cute. It's one of the ways women keep men entertained.

Dad recognizes his daughter's true inner nature (whereas Mom sees right through it). He understands that his girl is passionate rather than hysterical, brilliant rather than brainy. Dad often tolerates a degree of emancipation in a girl that he wouldn't stomach in Mom. Of course, he can rely on Mom to apply the brakes. He can play the good guy as long as she does her job and produces a feminine daughter. So he may encourage some assertiveness in a daughter, but only as long as it remains basically flirtatious and committed to getting her what she wants and only as long as it pleases him.

It turns out that the Princess, Daddy's Little Girl, is not really any better off. She may assert herself only in prescribed ways. She may not always have to serve others, as the Good Girl must, but she always has to please Dad in the long run. That seems O.K. as long as their interests coincide, but the terrible disappointment comes inevitably, as it does with Mom.

Dad and Mom always go off together. There always comes a time when Dad turns to Mom in a different way from the one he turns to his daughter. In the end, it's Mom he wants. His princess never wins the competition. She's never quite cute enough, however hard she works at it, however much she does to please him.

Dad likes his daughter to be attractive, but hates her to look cheap. It isn't easy to find that fine line between sexy and cheap, considering what most men find sexy and what girls are therefore exposed to in our culture. He always wants his daughter to stay either his little girl or a little lady. When he flirts with her, he does it as Prince Charming. He is ready to put her on the proverbial pedestal, and peek under her skirt. Nothing is too good for her, or even good enough, except him. She's his special girl, truly feminine, but a little spitfire underneath, the kind of woman a man would really fall in love with—once she's grown up. His girl loses his admiration when she becomes too obviously sexual. He puts her down for not knowing how to dress in a manner that appeals to him, for dressing to appeal to her peers—those she's interested in appealing to. He indicates that the way she looks when she's trying to please men other than Dad is a real turnoff. He makes it clear that she is going to have to choose between him and other men. He warns her, openly or by implication, that other men are only out to degrade her, to rip her off sexually.

So, as she grows up in his household, the Princess learns that she must please him first and foremost. He represents all men at first, but may eventually come to represent only a certain kind of man. Whether women marry men like their fathers depends on many factors. But it is probably safe to say that most of us marry men who either remind us of our fathers or who are specifically different from our fathers (or who remind us of our mothers, or are specifically different from our mothers). In other words, women marry a parent, or marry against a parent. In any case, the kind of relationship a woman has learned to have with her father is a model for the relationship she will have with her husband.

If Dad encouraged his daughter in feminine wiles, if he put her on a pedestal and kept her there, safe from male hands (except his own), and flirted with her while she was up there, she will probably end up with a tendency to be both sexually demanding and passive. If there is a lot of the Princess in her, he promised her, indirectly, that she would some day be the kind of woman he would fall in love with, and kept her waiting on her pedestal for the day he would choose her, finally releasing her into the arms of a husband to act as his proxy. The form of her demands depends on the relative strength of the Good Girl in her. The Princess part is overtly demanding, puts men down for not performing satisfactorily, reinforces their feelings of inadequacy because they aren't giving her what she needs or what she's been led to expect. But she isn't overtly angry; she's catty, makes cracks, has moods and outbursts. Pleasing Dad requires staying cute, performing well, never turning into a whining, complaining nag, regardless of how she feels. She must stay focused on him, on his needs, because filling them is the only way she knows to get what she needs. She learns she must please men, and what pleases them by trying to please Dad. Pleasing men requires staying sexy, the adult form of cute, without being "cheap" (unless he likes it that way). Cheap can mean any number of things, but mainly it means too active. Or at least it seems that way.

In the old family triangle Mom always won in the end. So somehow the daughter was not quite cute enough. And now she's not quite sexy enough to do the impossible. The men in her adult life are usually just as incapable of making it all up to her as Dad was. But she can't afford to express the full extent of her disappointment and anger to her husband any more than she could to her father. She has little reason to think she would be better off overtly rejected. So she turns the anger, displaces it, or rather focuses unremittingly on her legitimate anger at Mom, at other women, and downplays and ignores any sign of her legitimate anger at Dad and men. The affection she feels for her mother and her father can be genuine, but it is only part, not necessarily the most prominent part, of her whole emotional response to them. Suppressing the other, more hostile feelings, requires a great deal of energy. As time goes by, she learns to let up where she can, always keeping her eye on the main chance, on pleasing men. Men give her the support she needs—they would, that is, if she could only find, keep, train, or restrain the right one.

But that's only half the story. The Good Girl, living in Cinderella's father's house, has learned that any chance for getting Mom is seriously endangered by overt sexual activity. She can't afford to displease Dad because he could make her happy and safe or throw her out, but she can't afford to live without Mom as her lifeline. Staying with Mom means staying good, not even competing for Dad, losing him and any chance at being a star. Mom does not want a cute and sexy daughter; she wants one who is nice, devoted, faithful, sensitive, and co-operative. Cute and sexy are nice, useful tools for pleasing men, and woman's ultimate duty is to care for men and please them. Cute and sexy, especially, for its own sake or just because it gets us what we want, are not O.K. with Mom.

A Bad Girl calculates her chances openly and buys what she needs with her favors. A Bad Girl is cold and ruthless underneath, no matter how cute and sexy she may seem. Sooner or later men reject her, when the sexual passion is spent and they see her for what she really is! That's what the movies tell us, and what Mom has been led to believe. It is her earnest duty to pass this information on to her daughter by way of warning. Children are greedy and innocent; they have to be taught to be cautious and circumspect. Mom warns against sex: It is dangerous, can lead to pregnancy and ruin lives. Men won't marry women who aren't wife material; that lesson has to be learned and practiced. One false move can blow one's chances. Mom teaches that a woman needs a man. Sex is one way to get one and is important because it produces children, who are the real fulfillment of a marriage. But sex can also break up a marriage. It either keeps Dad regularly coming home with the bacon (or a major part of it) or hunting around out there in the jungle for cheap thrills. So Mom has to teach sexual attraction and how to deal with it once one has it. She stresses that sex is for men, not for women. Not that women can't enjoy and be moved by it as a sign of love, but lovemaking just for pleasure is cheap. And cheap is bad.

Sex is a lot of hormones causing chaos all over the place, which is all well and good for the young who have excess energy to burn or are newly in love. But when that part dies down one must settle into real marriage, which is mostly work. Mom expounds her philosophy with varying degrees of explicitness, bitterness, disdain, or disillusionment. She intimates that sex is, on the one hand, not a big deal for a woman and, on the other, the dark secret that keeps men and women involved with each other. She confuses her daughter, telling her not to get too close to it, not to get burned, not to try to understand it or experience more than necessary. Men have urges and have been ordained to find ways to express them. While some women lend themselves to this sort of thing, good girls don't.

Mom teaches distrust of women who use their sexuality overtly, either to trap men or to satisfy themselves. They steal men, blind them with sexual promises, suck them dry, and then discard them. (Or if they use the wrong guy *they* get discarded when they're old and don't get to live happily ever after.) Those women will die lonely and bitter. Men, of course, don't know any better than to be attracted to such women. But the Good Girl who endures and carries on will eventually be rewarded by her man's return to the family, where she can nurse his ego back into health. She learns that the appropriate object for her jealousy in relation to both parents is the loose woman out there.

The daughter has no hope of ever getting Mom if she's going to turn into one of those women and promises not to seriously explore her sexual feelings. She'll take Mom's word until marriage, when the risk of exploration is much reduced (her husband will help her figure out what's right and what isn't). He'll let her know how he likes her/it. She has learned what unchecked urges can do to men, how they're always turned on, always prey to sexual desire. Women aren't supposed to have such urges, only yearnings. If the Good Girl has an urge, or a feeling comparable to the description of men's urges, she worries about not being a real woman. And she *knows* that indulging in sex, either in deed or in feeling, is not being good.

Dad, meanwhile, in conjunction with Mom, warns and threatens his girl with tales about the "male beast." He exposes her to horror tales of rape, degradation, and dishonor in every cultural medium. Dad (and uncles, cousins, older brothers, and even younger brothers) confirm every rumor. They should know. They come back from the wars in the streets to warn about the bad guys: how they're interested only in cheap thrills, how that's all most men really want, how they don't respect a woman who succumbs to them, and how disgusted they are—morally repulsed—by a woman who actually likes the kind of sex they want to indulge in. Dad won't let his daughter out of the house without a warning of some kind, and neither will Mom. She may warn the daughter about her own imperfectly repressed impulses and he about the men she meets. She gets the message loud and clear that sex can only be defused (as it should be) through marriage and fidelity. Monogamy may be only an ideal for men, but it is absolute law for women.

Every now and then, a good girl may inadvertently fall in love with two men, or fall helplessly in love with another man after she's married. Then she must be torn between them and feel tremendous pain. She must not wish simply to sleep with both, possibly have a different kind of sexual relationship with each. She must burn with love, never with lust, for the other man and give up all sexual attraction to other men when she finally chooses between them. Being torn apart is punishment for emotional non-monogamy correctly and quickly resolved. If she vacillates and strings him along, trying to have her cake and eat it too, her reward will surely be far more terrible trouble.

Mostly, the Good Girl has to learn to accept the pain of constant sexual jealousy without fussing too much; a fuss will only drive her man into another woman's arms. She must repress her sexual curiosity early in childhood, postpone all sexual exploration until marriage, and then take it only where her sexually unknown husband wishes to. She may sometimes, on a

special occasion, enjoy herself in the throes of his sexual excitement but must never consciously experience lust without immediately transforming it into love/passion. Yet sex must be constantly on her mind, as the threat of rape or rivalry. Excitement
must become fear and jealousy, and eagerness or curiosity must
become vague yearnings and fantasies of romantic fulfillment.
She is allowed only to see herself walking hand in hand with her
knight in shining armor.

Dad's daughter, the Princess who hopes to walk hand in
hand with her father, can't afford any anger at him, at least
undue anger. She is, however, permitted to feel envy, jealousy,
and dislike of other women. So much of her identity is invested
in pleasing men, in being what men want her to be, that she
is very much at their mercy, even while acting less enduring and
long-suffering than the Good Girl in us. The Princess may express anger against Mom, vent it on lovers, friends, and children, but she pays for it by alienation from herself. She has to
choose men over women and identify with men to please them
expertly, to suppress the feelings they find unworthy, the interests they don't share, the intimacy based on common experience
rather than sexual negotiation.

The Princess in us has to choose against herself. She often
forgets that she *is* a woman, talks about women in general as
"they," but is rudely reminded that she is *not* a man, is not
really as good as a man, is not really accepted by men. She hates
woman because they are her rivals and men because they are her
exploiters. If she is angry at anyone, it is at herself and at women
like her.

Mom's daughter, the Good Girl, develops painful, debilitating physical symptoms, because she has no place at all to turn
her anger. She can't afford to feel any real anger at Mom, since
she is her lifeline. She must turn her anger inward, against herself. She must punish herself for feeling any anger at all, for
being imperfect, unfeminine. And she can't help trying to demonstrate her suffering, to get some credit and some safe, non-
sexual attention. She must turn her anger into pain and suffering. She must endure her own anger and bury it. She must
become a willing victim.

5
LOVE AND DANGER
Breaking the Incest Taboo

The family, like a sovereign nation, requires of all of its members, but especially its daughters, an oath of loyalty that affirms and idealizes all that transpires within its borders. No matter how little power the daughter has, she is expected to join the parents in promoting the rules and rituals that demonstrate family harmony and maintain family unity. To avoid exile, being thrust out of the emotional familiarity of the family, she has little choice but to take the oath and accept with it the consequences of hierarchy and inequality built into daily life.

Each family member is socially mandated to carry out the duties and meet the obligations of his or her role. The parents are entrusted with the responsibility of protecting their children from the dangers of their physically and socially powerless condition, and the children are supposed to trust and obey the adults who claim to act in their interest. Bound by love and duty, gratitude and fear, the daughter can only hope that her parents understand the boundaries of childhood and will not push her beyond her limits. Slowly and with a lot of reassurance, the daughter grows to trust the parents to act with restraint, tempering their absolute power with mercy and love.

Through the trials of infancy, the frustration of helplessness and the terror of being totally dependent on capricious but often loving tyrants, the daughter, like her brother, emerges into childhood with a greater sense of controlling the world. With the help of her mother she has mastered many of the small but essential tasks placed before her. She can feed herself, dress herself, help out, and play alone. She is getting to be a big girl and her mother takes pride in her forays into autonomy. Her fears of merging with her mother and her desire to do so are less persistent. She knows she is a separate person, can say no—at least sometimes—to assert her boundaries. Moving toward greater and greater freedom, although still dependent on her parents, the daughter can defend her interests and make some small claims to power.

Childhood, however, has undermined the infantile vision of her own power that allowed her to magically control her parents. Infancy was the golden age when her demands to be fed, cleaned, held, and reassured of her safety were miraculously met. But when her mastery of the world expands her parents don't respond to her demands in the same way. Paradise is lost, and the tables are turned. She must meet *their* demands for love and obedience and acknowledge her lack of control in relation to them. This embarrassing and often humiliating situation is more bearable when the daughter can escape the reality of her powerlessness. She feels stronger and less vulnerable when she believes she can reverse the social order and take the control that was wrested from her.

In her fantasies she lords it over her capricious caretakers, making them suffer for the neglect, injustices and betrayals she experiences. She pronounces them "guilty," meting out the punishment she thinks they deserve. Unwilling to accept her powerlessness, she is determined to gain some leverage in the family. As a counterforce to the parents' real and imagined omnipotence the daughter creates her own powerful agency. How can she trust them completely when they punish her unjustly, make demands that frighten and overwhelm her, and tell her that whatever happened to her was her own fault? If only she hadn't talked back, wet her pants, or refused to go to bed when she was told, she wouldn't have been spanked. She alone is responsible for pushing them to the edge of reason, for making them angry and withholding. They may explain cause and effect in six million ways but the daughter, the child, understands another logic, one mixed with her fears and wishes and her very own kind of interpretation. She believes she made them act badly, that she caused her own punishment.

One of the earliest lessons of daughterhood is that survival requires obedience. More than anything else, her parents want her to submit to their demands; and if she does, they say they love her. Reluctantly, the daughter allows herself to be commanded, coerced, and cajoled into acting out her parents' desires. Since they are her first beloved authorities, she finds it difficult to question their right to demand obedience. She may find the yoke of submission chafing and uncomfortable, but hopes that by fulfilling her part of the contract she will be rewarded by their good will and protection.

Yet the parents can interrupt and withhold the flow of nurturance and protection, depending on their mood. Although she depends on her mother, her female caretaker, to monitor the environment for signs of danger, the daughter has learned by many bitter experiences that she cannot always rely on her. The daughter can never fully accept this overwhelming disappointment and carries the transgressions of her mother like stigmata, her first wounds of injustice and repudiation, to be anguished over again and again. Not only did her mother abandon her, ignore her, and set limits, she gave her over to her father, like a sacrifice for punishment. The daughter feels betrayed by her mother's submission to his authority and wonders if her mother will defend her when she is really in danger.

The daughter fears the abuse of their power and does not understand why her parents victimize her. Maybe she *is* a bad child. When they yell at her to eat all the food on her plate, she gags, fearing their reactions to her disobeying and displeasing them. She must listen to them and try to please them so they will not desert her or hurt her or cast her out. They say they love her but only when she is good. Being good is her insurance premium for love, even though it requires her mute compliance and self-denial.

Her magical fantasies are, in fact, puny defenses against their real power over her existence. Her disobedience only angers these giants who do not always restrain their impulses to retaliate with a shove, a slap, or a piercing scream. More the slave than the master, no matter how many shuttle trips she makes between the reality of her powerlessness and the comfort of her fantasies for control, the daughter can never forget her place as a child; she can never be as powerful as adults. She has no choice but to comply, and as if to lighten the humiliation of her condition they tell her that they love her for it.

Her strongest attachments are to the parents who care for her and delineate her emotional map with their idiosyncratic expressions of affection. The affection and attention they show her, no matter how niggardly or arbitrary the bestowal, she experiences as love. The daughter accepts what they can afford to give and loves them completely, if always ambivalently. They are her dramatic extravanganza—stimulating, frightening, romantic, and dangerous. Being around them is always intense and full of mutual expectations.

The daughter also finds their company reassuring. When they are not making unreasonable demands on her, she feels safe with them and accepts the family as a haven and not an arena for her ritual submission. Her parents, if they observe the cultural rules for parenting, give her the security of knowing her appropriate place as a child, protect her from the consequences of feeling more powerful than she is, and help her with the frustration of not being grown up. If they show her the real limits of her power, no matter how deep her disappointment, she develops a realistic sense of her boundaries and capacities. If she believes them, she turns to them when she is frightened and out of control. No matter how much she resents their power, she needs their reminders that they will help her master the environment, which is often overwhelming and confusing.

Loving and fearing them, often in the same moment, the daughter wants to believe she is special to them, that they will do what is best for her. She pledges herself to them and lives by the oaths of loyalty they demand. In good faith she relinquishes control over her little body and greater will, believing they will honor and protect her vulnerability.

For better or worse she loves them and lives the dependency of childhood grateful for any proof of their affection, any sign of benevolence or recognition. She is relieved when they swallow their frustration with her many deficiencies and patiently wait for her to master the tasks they give her. Although they could physically hurt her at any moment, since she has no defenses against them, they spare her. The daughter is grateful that her parents are so tolerant of her and hopes she can make them happy in ways they want: getting good grades, helping with chores, never complaining. She will be good for them so that they will love and protect her. If she is bad she may lose their love or provoke their rage.

Any special attention, indulgence, or dispensation from the powerful parents encourages the daughter's dormant fantasy of omnipotence and reactivates her wish to merge with them in love. The shifting political alliances of the family triangle make the daughter a likely candidate for a special bond, her training for self-denial and compliance make her a good companion, confidante, and co-conspirator. She listens, does what she is told, is pleasant and smiles, and can be trusted with any number of secrets. Loyal, trustworthy and discreet, the daughter makes a good ally.

Yet why does a parent want an alliance with her? The daughter concludes that there is something special about her, her personality, her character, something. She feels she has been chosen, discovered, elevated from childhood obscurity to adult. While the emotional contractions and expansions at this new height are overwhelming at times, the loneliness of childhood is temporarily assuaged by the promise of a romantic connection with one of her parents.

A mother who makes this alliance with her daughter is often asking to be cared for, to be mothered by the child who reminds her of her own deprivation. A father who makes an alliance with the daughter is also asking to be cared for, but she is confused about what he wants from her since he is the supreme authority in the household, the Law, and already has someone to care for him. When the Father seeks an alliance with his daughter, she is honored that a person with his position and authority wants to spend time with her and be her friend. One woman recalls:

> After dinner, when my mother was clearing the table, Dad would give me that special look and I would get up to prepare a cup of tea for him. Then he and I moved onto the

sofa and he said, "Well, how was my Princess today? Tell me everything that happened." Then he asked me to prepare his bath and lay out the soap and towels. I never wondered why I was chosen. I was delighted to be able to serve him.

Unaware of the implications of her premature elevation to the status of adult, the daughter believes she is better than her siblings and perhaps more appealing than the excluded spouse. She feels special and chosen. She secretly nourishes a belief in her own equality and the mutuality of interest with her parent.

Mixed with her passion for him is a broad and deep stream of guilt. Jealous of her mother's prior claim to this man but delighted that he seems to have chosen her over the mother, she can only conclude that she has won the competition with her mother. Guiltily triumphant, the daughter spins a fantasy of romantic love that endures and flourishes. She buries her guilt and fears of maternal revenge, dreaming of one day going off with Dad and leaving Mom behind.

Unaware of her daughter's wishes to be chosen over her, Mom is relieved to share the burden of serving and entertaining Dad. She has instructed her daughter in the proper attitudes of deference and demeanor toward the father, preparing the daughter to respect his authority and comply with his wishes. The mother advises the daughter not to refuse or resist because disobedience causes family conflict and makes life worse for Mom. If the daughter angers her father or flouts his authority, she may escape punishment, but her mother will suffer. The daughter who is bound by love to make life for her mother as pleasant as possible learns quite early that there are times her father must get his way if the family is to survive and her mother is to endure.

While the daughter yearns to win her father from her mother, she feels their alliance must be kept secret. Her mother has made it clear to her that the father is a tyrant and a baby, often not worth the trouble she puts up with, the abuse she takes. She says that one day she might leave him, but not now, maybe when the daughter is older. Knowing how her mother feels about the father, the daughter decides not to tell her about the man she knows, the man who gives her so much pleasure. She doesn't want her mother to be hurt or jealous, and she doesn't want her mother to leave.

Caught between the emotional crosscurrents of her own longings to be special, to be chosen by her father, and her fears of rejection, abandonment, and undeserved punishment from her mother, the young daughter regards her father's requests for her time and energy as both pleasurable and frightening. As the most powerless member of the family triangle, she comes to understand that by pleasing her father she will have an ally and benefit from his power.

The father is the ultimate authority in the household, inspiring fear and longing in his daughter. He has the right to punish and discipline his children as he sees fit but often reaches out to his daughter, drawing her close to him. She feels protected and stimulated. Even when she feels a strange tension between them, the quickening of his speech or the insistence of his glance, the daughter doesn't understand the meaning of her father's feelings toward her. Her curiosity may be aroused by his new interest in her, his manifestations of joy when they are alone together, but as a child she hopes only that she will be safe with the man she loves and fears.

At first the father-daughter alliance is suffused with excitement and romance. He wants to take his daughter camping, or to the ball game, or teach her to work in the garden, or identify birds in the woods near the house. He says he wants her to be like him, to share the activities that give him pleasure. He tells her she is very important to him, that he and she are a team, maybe even dares to say her mother wouldn't understand their shared interests. He is seducing her, and she feels her heart fill with pleasure.

Becoming the object of his undivided attention, receiving his caresses and kisses, being spoken to softly and gently, unlike his tone to her mother, make the daughter aware of something different about their "new" relationship. She feels cared for, loved, and appreciated, and wishes the boundaries that divided them would dissolve so she could melt into him and never be alone again. His incestuous feelings and her own find a limited if not benign expression in these acts of romantic love, acts that will be replaced by future distance as they become more conscious of the taboo on incest.

There is no general agreement as to the original function of the incest taboo but it is clear that good parenting requires protecting daughters from demands for sexual service by fathers and brothers. No matter how deprived the father feels, society asks him to allow his daughter to grow through childhood without sexualizing his bond with her and placing his needs before her own. When a father decides to seduce the daughter, crossing the cultural barrier of the incest taboo, he ends his daughter's childhood, depriving her of the parenting she needs. As he transforms the content of childhood, he ushers her into adult heterosexual negotiation. Because he has the power, and because of her own mixed emotions, the daughter believes she cannot refuse.

Incest occurs whenever a father makes himself responsible for his daughter's sexual initiation. His desire to manage her exchange of "innocence" with "experience" may consist of his asking her to touch him, to masturbate him, to let him touch her. It may start when she is three or five or ten, last through puberty and into adolescence, or stop when she looks frightened or angry. He may only want to touch her once or create elaborate rituals of seduction and sexual fantasy that last for years, interspersed with the "normal" routines of growing up. No matter how often the incestuous father demands his daughter's assistance, no matter how the details of his acts differ, he violates the daughter by confusing the nature of child-parent relationships, colonizing her body for his own use.

A father who makes an overt alliance with his daughter causes mixed feelings in her. Since adults and children compete with each other for the scarce resources of nurturance and approval, the boundaries between the socially powerful and powerless often become blurred and confused. Although all must cohabit and cooperate, each hopes to win something special from the other, to feel less deprived and dependent. When the inherently unstable triangular situation triggers overwhelming feelings of deprivation in one or both parents, the cultural rules for parenting are placed in jeopardy, and the child is in danger of being abused.

Any daughter would be pleased that Daddy wants to spend time alone with her. She likes their rides in the car or their secret meetings when Mommy leaves the house. It is exciting to play hide-and-seek and have him tickle her when he finds her. The father who acts on incestuous desires adds another dimension to their game. He may want to kiss her and touch her in places she has known only through her own masturbation, saying he knows it will feel good, that it is a special place with a delicious tingle.

One daughter remembers being four or five when her father asked her if she wanted to touch his penis. She was in the front seat of his old Dodge, and they were out on one of their country rides without her mother, who preferred to stay home to catch up on her chores and probably have some freedom from being a wife and mother. She was ecstatic to be alone with him, but she can't remember everything that went on.

> He presented his request as an educational thing. He was going to show me something I had never seen before and I was very curious. I don't remember having any sexual feelings myself. I thought of it as helping him, pleasing him. But I was not frightened in the beginning.

> I was an only child. I was lonely and our relationship was a friendship, an attachment, affection. I don't remember my mother kissing or holding me; certainly she must have sometime. I don't know if I agreed to please him because of that or because I was initially curious.

What meaning can her father's desire to give her a sexual education have to a daughter? How can she make sense of her father's demand for her to please him through mute participation in acts strangely meaningful but remotely understood?

When the daughter recollects childhood, her memories of incest have a dreamy quality. While many sexual acts are crystal clear, reassuringly comprehensible, most of her emotional states are opaque and often resist clarification in language. The daughter has sense memories, traces of feelings that don't seem to fit the story she has been told or the one she tells herself about her special secret and how she felt about him.

In breaking the incest taboo the father lets the daughter know he will go "that far" for her. By violating the taboo that separates men and society from animals and nature, he admits that society's moral opprobrium and his wife's jealous fury mean little in the face of his desire. The daughter knows there is something wrong, since it must remain secret, but being chosen by the most powerful adult in her family pleases her and the secret sexual alliance makes her feel special.

Since she is a native speaker of the family's language the daughter knows that in making his alliance with her into a sexual initiation, her father has chosen to address her in the language of love. This jars the daughter's sense of propriety and her daily routine of dependency and powerlessness. He talks to her as an equal, telling her she has something he needs and wants, that she, his young daughter who wants him to be the all-powerful, must help him. Her father turns the tables on her, promising her all his love, telling her he is giving something very important, that will serve her later in life; he is teaching her to be a woman. Not only must she passively allow her father to pleasure himself through her, she must depend on him for her own pleasure. In exchange for her silence he promises to delight her.

He speaks to her as an ally, coconspirator, telling her that their shared secret is potent enough to tear down their house. They are bound to each other by an act so misunderstood that it can never be mentioned or acknowledged overtly. He whispers not to tell Mother: She wouldn't understand, would be jealous about being left out of their game, would be angry with her daughter and yell, maybe leave. He pleads. The secret is obviously very important and the daughter is thrilled by the power he gives her. As partners in crime, they are two outlaws in disguise, acting normal and in role most of the time, but returning to a secret life where his desire transforms the daughter's social powerlessness into erotic power.

Incest creates an impossible situation for the daughter who must lead a double life. She cannot tell lest her mother's anger destroy the daughter's liaison with the father and perhaps the family itself. The daughter believes that if Mother discovers her part in the game, she will blame Daughter, and secret trysting and secret pleasure will come to a dramatic and conclusive end. The father's aggressive seduction, hostile to both mother and child, could, if revealed, leave the daughter with no ally, perhaps two enemies, and the mother with the wrenching task of choosing between defense of her man and protection of her daughter. When they successfully fool the mother by their secrecy, they save her from having to act on potentially intolerable choices.

Incest creates an impossible situation for the mother whose social powerlessness and psychological dependency make her willing to bolster the father's authority to protect his position, thereby protecting her own. If she confronts him with her suspicions, he might leave and if he leaves she may be unable to care for her children. Without his income to maintain the family, the mother faces certain poverty. She is therefore hooked by raw economics and intense emotions. She too has been somebody's daughter and learned that one must please men to survive.

Mother is the only household member who has the socially defined moral responsibility to enforce the incest taboo in the nuclear family. She is required to police the family for signs of sexual negotiation between any of its members; she must protect her daughter and control her husband's impulses. Her role forces her to face the possibility of incest because if it occurs she is held responsible.

A wife rarely thinks of her husband as a man who could confuse his parental role of nurturing the emerging autonomy of a child with that of a heterosexual man who asks his young daughter to be his secret lover. What wife can bear the thought of a husband willing to ignore the cultural taboo against a father's sexually initiating a daughter into adult heterosexual status? She doesn't understand the kind of man who would place his sexual needs on the narrow border between nature and culture. Could he not understand the taboo or just pretend not to? Or does he see his daughter as property to use as he pleases?

The daughter, the victim of her inevitable child's lack of power, hopes her mother will challenge and defeat her father's authority by discovering their tryst and restoring her sense of safety so suddenly shattered by his repeated caresses. She wants Magic Mommy, her first love and current source of hope, to rescue her. Although the daughter has been sworn to secrecy by promises and threats, she hopes her mother will protect her, as she has done in the past.

The daughter wonders why her mother doesn't sense what is happening, why she isn't suspicious, why she doesn't try to divert his attention from her. Could it be that Mother has authorized his behavior? Is her silence and lack of curiosity a signal to the daughter that she is willing to share her husband? Or is she willing to sacrifice her daughter for her own security and reputation? Long after the incident has occurred daughters find it almost impossible to ask their mothers if they knew.

There was a time when I thought that she might have known since she never intervened in anything that my father wanted to do. She would try to work around him, helping me on the sly, but never openly contradicting him or choosing my well-being over his. Because she was very cold and strict and never mentioned sex, I thought that she might have given the job of sex education to my father.

When I had intercourse with him for the first time, after five years of masturbation and fellatio, I explained the blood to my mother by saying that I got my period and asked her to get me sanitary napkins. She asked me no questions. I assumed she didn't want to know. But now I think she didn't even suspect what was going on.

There was no point in telling her anything since she wasn't interested in my real life except if she thought she could finally make me into the prissy kind of girl she liked. I preferred to forget the whole thing since there wasn't much she could do anyway. She wasn't going to leave him, she didn't have her own money or a job. And she probably wouldn't have believed me ... she might have thought that I was boasting.

The possibility that the mother knows and does nothing is excruciating for the daughter so she denies that such a possibility exists. She casts her mother as a poor innocent, fooled by her daughter's excellent acting and generous protective instincts. The sacrifice made of her body, her childhood and her autonomy becomes the daughter's responsibility and the mother is exonerated before she can be blamed. In the daughter's eyes, the mother is the *real* victim of incest.

During the time I was having sex with my father I wanted to protect my relationship with my mother. We didn't have a warm bond but I felt that if she knew she would be hurt. I wanted to protect her.

I always felt that my mother needed protection since she acted like I was the man of the house. She would ask me to figure out things that were just too complicated for her poor little head. She had a lot of poor-me routines but when I was a kid I never doubted that my role was her protector and not vice versa. If she knew my father was "playing with me" I was afraid that she would kick him out and be left without his economic support.

Protecting the mother is the daughter's rationalization for the loss of her mother's protection and a cover for her own anger. She is angry because her mother didn't know or intervene. But few incest survivors blame their mothers for allowing incest to go on, insisting instead that it was their Good Girl duty to take care of her by not upsetting her. Since she must lose her mother to please her father, she resigns herself to isolation and quiet despair. She believes that she must stand alone, without her mother and give up her desire to be saved. She tries to leave all the hints she can but her mother turns away and the daughter concludes that perhaps Mom doesn't want to know. With no real options at hand, she keeps her own counsel, rationalizing her isolation as the fulfillment of some greater goal—saving the family, protecting her younger siblings from the father, or ensuring her mother's sanity. Incest is the cross she has to bear; by facing each day like a martyr, she accepts her fate and endures.

Incest requires a young girl to take on precociously the psychological and social attributes of femininity. Like other heterosexual relations based on unequal power, incest is one her father romanticizes and presents as an act of love. The child's sense of social powerlessness is confounded by her father's insistence that her erotic power draws him to her. Their secret requires her to be feminine: cooperative, altruistic, enduring, and above all, compliant. He defines the situation and expects her to accept her role with pleasure. While she protects him from exposure, she must nurture him and attend to his interests, think of his safety before her own, obey and enjoy his authority, love him, and submit to his demands.

Unprotected by her mother and sworn to secrecy by her father, the daughter is afraid to refuse his access to her body, of not giving him what he wants. As he enjoys the right to demand his pleasure, so has he the right to punish her resistance. Her childish sense of grandiosity is no real defense against the situational inequality that enforces her absolute helplessness. She can't control him and, although she may feel responsible, she didn't *make* him initiate this sexual exchange and she can't make him stop. He claims his rights to her flesh, by virtue of being a father, as well as a heterosexual man. Afraid of losing the one parent who shares her secret and loves her for her silence and compliance, the daughter becomes emotionally dependent upon her father-turned-lover for her sense of self-esteem and security.

I know that this will sound strange to you but I still believe that my father cared about me very much and perhaps loved me more than my mother. What he did was wrong but he never stopped loving me and that was important to me.

Through her initiation into an incestuous relationship with her father, the daughter thinks she will have an ally for life, someone who will love her and be indebted to her for not exposing him. He entrusts her with the awesome responsibility of maintaining his innocence and protecting him as well as her mother. As the coconspirator, powerless to change her situation, the daughter uses her limited autonomy to serve her father's needs, no matter how inappropriate. She must remain silent for self-protection and to protect the adults and the siblings who depend on her muteness for their ongoing sense of family unity.

As a sexual initiation, incest carries within it the culture's stereotype of idealized romantic pairings: the older, more experienced male, gentle and loving, with the sexually innocent ingenue. He is tough in the public world but privately, with the woman he loves, he is gentle and considerate. The father frequently plays this role with his daughter. The daughter must play her part in turn, innocent of the significance of his demands, willing to please, without cynicism or anger. If she acts the role as her father wishes, she must preserve the appearance of goodness and innocence even when his sexual demands become more insistent and unpleasant. Asked to be a very good girl and a very bad girl, the daughter is placed in a schizophrenic position, she is fragmented by having to be a traitor in her mother's house, her father's secret concubine, and a dutiful Good Girl protecting her mother from pain. Her concrete situation is romanticised—love is rationalized as a motive for invasion. Excommunicated from childhood, not yet an adult woman, she is set up not to feel violated, but cherished; not to feel overwhelmed and out of control but special, not to resist but to accept her fate, that "Father Knows Best."

The daughter who continues to believe, as most incest survivors do, that she aroused her father's passion and provoked incest by her desire to be close to him is convinced that there is something powerful and evil in her. After all, she reasons, she was able to draw this man—otherwise so responsible—across the cultural frontier that was barricaded by awe and disgust. She thinks her body contains a secret power to make men transgress the basic rules of civilization, courting contempt and social retaliation. Having given up so much to please him, she may retain the image of herself as the seductress whose allure makes her irresistible to the one man who promised her love.

He started touching me when I was only eleven. I remember thinking that I must have had breasts and a very sexy attitude to make him do that. But when I looked at the family album, I realized that I was just a skinny, gawky, and very shy looking little girl. For years I thought that I caused him to come on to me.

Guilt and fear have not been routed from daughters' recollections of childhood seduction. "Perhaps he was doing it for me like he said, perhaps he was giving me pleasure and getting nothing for himself. Perhaps I was getting more love than my mother. It must have been my fault." The daughter who concludes that she is guilty for her father's actions has not yet recognized the separation that exists between the will of an adult and that of a child. In refusing to acknowledge her powerlessness she holds on to the notion that her thoughts and her father's are mystically and mutually one. If she cannot accept her very real victimization she will never have to lose this grandiose and infantile view of heterosexual relations or give up her desire to merge with a man.

Incest usually occurs at point in a girl's life when magical thinking is operative. Her egocentric view of the world encompasses her father's wishes, which she translates into her own. She feels that she causes or controls events around her. Carried into adulthood, this magical thinking is dysfunctional. Children whose parents help them understand how finite and minuscule a child's control of events really is, become aware of the real and limited options available to them in social situations. A father who exploits his daughter by encouraging her to distort reality and accept responsibility for adult actions triggers endless confusion about boundaries and events and the daughter's ability to control them.

In her life outside the household the daughter tries to act like other girls her age, never revealing the knowledge and experience of heterosexuality that she considers her mark of difference. She thinks she's the only one. She continues the charade that has ensured her survival and kept the family together. But she often suffers, not sure the boundaries are real, uncomfortable with saying no, unable to make firm decisions or stand up for herself. She renounced her will when she agreed to keep the secret; she isn't sure that she is entitled or able to assert her will again. She fears having to submit to the demands of other adults and keeps a low profile, hesitant to say what she means for fear that the secret will leak out of her mouth. She tells no one and hopes that the traces of incest will disappear with the other traumas of childhood.

For years there have been no words to describe the daughter's experience of incest since the subject was never broached in social language. Feelings buried so deep and so long come to the surface loaded with sediments of pain and humiliation. The emotional charge of events is detonated when the daughter remembers the transgression and gives it its proper name—incest. She is surprised by other peoples' revulsion and feels defiled—an object of pity. They look at her suspiciously or shake their heads with sadness. They require a sign of her innocence, some expression of her hatred of the man, contempt that equals theirs for his terrible abuse of power. They see her as a victim, but at first she doesn't see herself in that light. After all, what happened? She followed his lead—submitted, as she had many times before to his demands for affection and gratification—and feels that it could have been worse, he didn't rape or beat her, she is grateful that he loved her. She denies that she was powerless as a girl and wonders why she didn't resist, since everybody says what he did was abominable. She finds it difficult to name herself a victim, to remember her despair, and is unable to accept as perversion what he said he did in the name of love. But few incest survivors can remember being openly angry at their fathers' requests for sexual service.

In my teenage diaries I was venomous, to the point of rage toward him, but the anger was never about the sexual activity directly. I was angry at the restrictions he was placing on my life with my friends. He didn't want me to have friends at all, since he wanted me to do things with him. I wasn't even allowed to participate in sports after school because he wanted me at the dinner table precisely at five and not a minute later. When I wanted to go away to school, he said high school was good enough for me since I would just marry some local boy and settle down.

From the time he showed me his penis, through the weekly episodes of making me watch him masturbate to ejaculation in our cramped tile bathroom, to his touching my clitoris and finally to his successful and not so successful attempts at penetration when I was thirteen, I felt sure that he cared about me. Even though he was not a very verbal man, I am convinced that he did and I don't blame him even though I know that what he did was wrong.

Some recognize their ambivalence.

Do you believe it? I thought he was doing me a favor, making me come and not asking to do anything for him. I never understood what men got out of it or why sex was so all important but I sure didn't think he would stop when I told him to . . . but he did. Then I was worried that I took so long in asking . . . I knew what he was doing was wrong but it felt good . . . that's a hell of a dilemma for a kid . . . and for an adult too.

However, some can remember the fear.

My father started touching me when I was six years old. He would tiptoe into my room while Mom was downstairs cooking dinner and say that he wanted to play with me because it would make him feel better. I was scared but I had to do what he wanted me to do. In my house nobody could talk back to him. I felt helpless and tried to avoid him. I broke into a cold sweat when I heard him come home from work and I avoided him by playing outside as long as I could. As soon as he could, he'd corner me and put his hand inside my panties. I began to have terrible nightmares and could never look him in the eye. I was terrified of him all the time I was growing up.

If incest is part of the daughter's early relationship with her father, she may believe long after the event that she was sexually irresistible and that she was at fault for letting it go on as long as it did. As guilty as she feels for not ending it sooner, she feels guiltier for not wanting to end it, torn between losing her father and the affection and pleasure he wanted to give her, and *did* give her, on some erotic level. She finds it confusing that incest which evokes disgust, pity, and fury in so many people, seemed so normal and inevitable, a part of her growing up. She agrees that it was terrifying and horrible, but she never talks about the pleasure. That is her final secret and her ultimate shame.

In spite of having given up so much for her father, the daughter tries to protect him from her anger and disappointment. She insists that he really loved her, that no one but she could fathom that fact, that she was the only one in the family who understood or knew him. From her defiled and exalted place of the family martyr, she had a view of him that was unavailable to her mother or even her other sisters. She knew him when he was gentle and romantic, soft and tender, and believes she saw a side of him that he exposed to no one else. She wants to protect him and preserve her unusual status in her own eyes.

Refusing to acknowledge her suffering she cherishes a romantic vision of their relationship as one of star-crossed lovers. It is much more painful to face her victimization. If she refuses to give up her infantile view of the heterosexual romance between father and daughter, she carries an unfulfilled desire to have her father openly declare his love for her. She believes he is afraid to speak openly about their love. She decides to read his mind and in so doing make her thoughts his motivations. She continues to protect him and herself from the grief and pain that still reside in her body and dreams.

In placing her parents' need for protection before her own, the daughter acts the family martyr. She refuses to place responsibility on her parents for the agonizing isolation she suffered, and she vows never to confront them with what went on. She buries her deprivation, resigned to the fact that her parents will not support her desires for autonomy. Daddy's Princess and Mommy's Good Girl never speaks about what happened.

After incest stops the daughter may be confused about retaining her father's concern and care. He dominated and possessed her child's body through his power and privilege, but she interprets his advances as an exhilarating mixture of love and control. He taught her to be an extension of his will and desires, a handmaiden to his pleasure, flesh of his flesh, and source of his happiness. She represses the bad feelings she experienced to protect herself from emotions of rage and grief. She cherishes the times he said he needed her, that she was special to him, that she was his wonderful little girl, that she brought him to life. When incest is over and the intensity of her secret love affair cools, the daughter is relieved, but also sad and regretful.

After the daughter leaves home, renouncing her father to seek a more acceptable and equal partner in love and sex, she may find it difficult to replace him and the precocious mutuality she believes they shared. While it is difficult for the daughter to leave the family in which she has undergone her initiation to heterosexuality, she must ultimately observe the demands of her society. At adolescence she is expected to take up the "normal" life of a young woman, dating, with the goal of falling in love. But that life is a pale reflection of the passion and intrigue she experienced in the nuclear family, and she is unsure of her ability to follow the new rules and still guard her secret.

The daughter has proved she can attract a man and be desirable. She is no longer a virgin, either physically or psychologically, and therefore is emotionally out of sync with her agemates. Who could replace her father? What selfish, clumsy teenage boy will understand her precocious sexual sophistication and treat her with care? Although she has confirmed her femininity in the family, she seeks affirmation of her "normalcy" in teenage social life.

Because incest involves giving up control of the right to say no, she experienced it as an invasion, whatever the mixture of pain and pleasure it contained. Her father's insistent demands had an obsessive quality that remains with the daughter when she contemplates future sexual liaisons. Her mute terror is reactivated by thoughts of her future obligations as a heterosexual woman.

Some daughters react by placing themselves only in situations that give them complete control over sexual negotiations and participation in sexual acts.

I was shy and withdrawn, with a very poor self-image, when I started dating in high school. I found all the boys very boring. When I met the man I married he asked for a kiss on the first date. I told him that if he wanted to see me again he could not ever try to touch me. I set the guidelines and they were followed for the next five years.

My husband turned out to be very passive and his sexual needs were not that great, so he never pressed. At the time I thought that he was just respecting the rules I had made and that from his point of view he had married a virgin.

Many women hide their prior sexual relationships with their fathers from their husbands, fearing jealous accusations of badness and rejection.

I too felt that I had never had sex before, since I had tried very hard to block my father and our relationship out of my mind. By the time I was married I felt like a virgin, but I didn't really know how to get pleasure from a mutual sexual relationship. Throughout the time with my father I had been passive, only trying to please him, letting him do whatever he wanted, acting as if I had no desires of my own. He ran the show and I watched. For these reasons having a two-way loving relationship appeared to be almost impossible.

Pledged to secrecy for life, the daughter establishes new relationships, but always on the foundation of the original one. Never telling her husband, her own children, or friends or lovers or ministers or anybody, the daughter holds on to her past shame with a tenacity she doesn't understand and cannot question. She holds on to the child's responsibility not to tell on her parents, as if the events she lived through and survived still required her obedient silence. She believes her power to reveal could still destroy the very people she has protected these many years.

After incest the daughter's relationship to adult hetero-sexual men and her own desires for sexual activity are never free from elements of reaction. Because incest invaded her boundaries, one daughter finds it difficult to pursue sexuality without fear and anger. She may look for a man who will make no sexual demands or who will let her call the shots, make the decisions, control sexual exchanges. She looks for safety.

Another incest survivor may believe she has no right to control, that she must stay a little girl to get protection and affection. Psychologically prevented from identifying with her mother, blocked from a relationship she needed, the daughter has an exaggerated sense of dependence in relating to men and the world. Her needs for physical affection having been over-stimulated, men's attention in any form assures her that she is acceptable and lovable.

Yet no incest victim ever feels completely safe. Confused by her desires and wishes, she wonders if she will be continu-ally forced to give up control, to do for others as she had to for her father and mother. Her interactions with authorities leave her feeling like a small child, believing her interests can be defended by someone else. Since her dependence on her father has not been restructured or broken, she may try to re-place him with lovers (men or women), to keep from feeling so alone. Sexually overstimulated in childhood, the daughter usually equates receiving approval with giving sexual service.

She knows that her ambivalence toward her father must be transformed if she wants to relate to men as a "normal" woman. Some daughters deal with this conflict by becoming obsessively promiscuous, testing their lovability with every man they meet. They frequently dull the pain and fear of incest associated with each sexual encounter by drinking, smoking dope, or taking pills. By narcotizing herself the daughter at-tempts to participate in sexual situations without experiencing her old fears. Other incest survivors try to regain control by replaying seduction and reversing the roles. By pursuing men and seducing them, the daughter feels more entitled to sexual pleasure.

But sexual pleasure is often denied these daughters. Their bodies, used in childhood for their fathers' needs, seem to have gone dead; they experience few orgasms and little release of tension or pleasure. Something feels broken inside and the past sits heavily on their bodies as they try to feel something, something that will make them "normal," like other women.

The irony for the daughter who has lived with the secret of incest is that her experience is merely an exaggeration of the daughter's dangerous condition of vulnerability in the family. What has been writ large in incest is the father's absolute authority, the mother's complicity, and the daughter's sacrifice to the heterosexual power struggle of her parents. Her dependency, sexual curiosity, and love for her father have been harnessed by the needs of two adults who betrayed her trust and made the family triangle a literal exploitation of unfulfilled needs.

The difference between wish and reality, pleasure and pain, childhood and adulthood, love and violation remains problematic for the daughter as she moves beyond the confines of the nuclear family. Questioning her complicity in incest, she carries with her the guilt that should be her parents' burden. Her initiation into adult femininity and heterosexuality is not a ritual confirmed by culture or shared with a community. No words of celebration or rejoicing are spoken when the daughter is treated like a woman and her father acts like her lover. Instead she feels her secret is shameful, sinful, and terribly wrong.

Although incest is often preceded and followed by many acts of tenderness and affection, something shatters when a father ignores the limits of parenting and power. Like other abuses of privilege visited upon the oppressed, incest mystifies the social relations of dependency in the family and names the daughter, as the most powerless member by virtue of her age and gender, responsible for her own abandonment and loss of autonomy.

LOVE AND DANGER: THE INCEST TABOO

Every daughter would like to believe that her father would restrain himself, would never entertain reprehensible thoughts, and would never violate her. But the truth of gender relations in the family and the world is that men, because they have power as men and as patriarchs, can extract obedience from their dependents and act as they wish with little fear of discovery or retribution. No daughter can defend herself alone against the powerful authority her father represents. He can be an outlaw, transgressing the taboo that maintains both the social and moral order if he so chooses. Safely hiding out in the hills of the isolated nuclear family, the father is the bandit king and his peasants must tolerate his acts of terrorism lest he wreak havoc upon them. Protected by his wife and idealized by his daughter, the father holds sway and rules without fear of revolt. No daughter can challenge what society has allowed to men, and no daughter can be sure that her vulnerability will be protected.

6

RAPE AND THE RITUALS OF HETEROSEXUALITY

The daughter who wants to be considered a success as a heterosexual woman must be willing to reproduce a life of domesticity in broad outline no different from the one her mother created. She must find a man to marry her and give her children. If she succeeds she receives the rewards that society offers to "good" women and takes her place alongside generations of "normal" women. If she fails, she bears the stigma of deviance and the pity of others who assume there is something wrong with her.

The daughter leaves home hoping to fulfill the mandate of femininity—to find a man. Leaving the physical and emotional intimacy of the family, she enters a world of strangers from whom she seeks acceptance and approval, yearning to fulfill her desires for pleasure and autonomy. If she wins the love of a man, she justifies her departure from the family and returns with her most important goal achieved.

Although she may agree with her mother that marriage is her ultimate feminine fulfillment, the daughter has an agenda of her own. Once free from parental surveillance and restrictions, she hopes to take risks and test herself in ways that were forbidden to her while she lived in her parents' home. The nonfamilial world offers her the possibility of adventures and romance as an exciting new ground in which to take control of her life after her long apprenticeship in self-denial and compliance.

The world beyond the family described to the daughter as the source of her affirmation, the arena of her quest for completion, is presented as dangerous. The daughter is cautioned about the consequences of not being vigilant about her safety or not being wary of the traps laid for her. The mother contrasts the domestic world of safety with the danger of territories that lie beyond her control. She suggests to the daughter that she marry as soon as she can and return to the home, where, like her mother, she will derive her legitimate power. Her future adventure should be short-lived, and the daughter should reenter her proper domain as quickly as possible. The mother interprets the foray into the world of strangers as a dangerous but necessary test of the daughter's heterosexual potential.

From the daughter's perspective the mother's fears are usually exaggerated. She wonders if her mother is manipulating her into repeating her mother's life to alleviate doubts the mother may feel about her own choices. She is tired of being a good listener, her mother's confidante and co-worker, the sensible and reassuring ear that hears all but is never asked to state her own concerns or confusions. The daughter is more than ready to exchange her mother's renditions of domestic safety for the excitement of new social and emotional challenges in the world. Fortified with the resources of youth, with energy, trust, and a strong desire for new experiences, she wants to know herself in ways not nurtured in the family.

What Mother calls danger her daughter calls life, and daughters are drawn toward life with a determination that refuses to observe the limits set for them. The daughter desires to discover her real self, not through service but in self-directed choice. In trying to discover her identity, she pushes the imposed limits. She breaks curfews, travels alone without an "escort," and experiments with drugs, liquor, and/or sex. She wants better odds than her mother has given her. Before she takes on the mantle of domesticity she wants to have a good time, to have lovers, friends, and colleagues. In short, leaving the family offers the daughter the chance to test her autonomy and her strengths in the world.

The daughter has her own reasons for hooking a man. The slights, disappointments, and defeats she has suffered in the family push her to find a man who will repair the damage. She believes that once out of the family she will become visible as herself for the first time. All that is unique and special about her will be affirmed in love. Until she discovers her special man she will withstand her loneliness and hunger to be known and loved, and do what she must to become a woman who is attractive to men.

As the daughter sets out to make her way she reassures her parents that she will be careful and promises not to take chances with strange men, to write, and to call. Yes, she will try to be the girl they groomed her to be: She will appear fragile, but secretly nourish her strength, accept what may not please her but try to get what she wants, be flexible and not rigid, and above all, do the best with what she's got.

Mother transmits a formula for heterosexual success that appears to be crude and demeaning—she calls it "realistic." The daughter is assured that in the family she is loved for who she is, but with men, she will have to work on herself and try to make the most of what she has; she should try to look as appetizing as she can. Once she evaluates her assets (good legs, straight teeth, small feet, graceful hands) and her flaws (acne, poor posture, breasts that are too big or too small) she must work on them, hide, refine, mask and disguise that which might reduce her chances of winning a man. If all else fails, the daughter knows that she can get pregnant and hope he will marry her. But the message from her mother is don't frighten men away. Without doing *too much* she should make herself safe territory for men.

But is she allowed to draw men to her? Can she ensure that men will find her attractive by deploying her sex appeal or is it too dangerous to be overtly desirous of sexual response? The message the mother gives the daughter about using her body to attract men always avoids direct discussion of sexual negotiation. While she is mandated to use her sex appeal to attract a man, acting on her sexual desires to experience self-authored pleasure is sternly forbidden. If she wants sex she must wait until all circumstances point to success. In other words, she must wait until she is sure she will not be considered bad. The daughter's goodness is affirmed when she is chosen.

To be considered good, the daughter must distinguish herself from the bad girls who are considered wild, sexually precocious, and likely to get hurt. She must cultivate a demeanor of modesty and naiveté. She must turn away if the conversation turns to the dangerous area of sex and assume a stance of sexual ignorance or indifference to show men (and other women) that she is not too sophisticated, or too interested in what has been taboo for her to pursue with a sense of entitlement. She must accept men as the rightful initiators and managers of all heterosexual encounters; to get their respect she must suppress her sexual longings and desires to act, substituting a presentation of self that underscores her reticence, hesitation, and helplessness. If the daughter can accomplish this task, made immeasurably easier by her on-the-job training as a Princess, she may convince men that she is good and deserves their protection, care, and fidelity. It is not surprising that the daughter accepts this stance, which gives men control over sexual and social exchanges and makes her more feminine, thus more desirable.

The daughter believes that in the face of potential sexual harm her best protection is to repress her own desires and sexual longings. She is afraid even to recognize the strength of her sexual appetites since acknowledging erotic passion makes her question her goodness. She wants to see herself, and be seen, as morally pure, unconcerned with sexual feelings—that is, good. She allies with society and defends the double standard that calls for her to participate actively in her own repression. She claims she is not interested in sex—the domain of men—that she wants only to have fun and fall in love.

As her sexual hungers are denied, the daughter transforms her desires into a more acceptable search for romance with the man of her dreams. She feels safer thinking of having sex with a man who has promised to love and protect her, even if it is from the "dangers" of sexual autonomy. If she finds him, if he finds her, she will give him the gift of her body and allow him to possess her in the name of love. This man will not judge her by her desires or think less of her for having them. If she finds him she will be able finally and completely to give up control over her sexual longings and relax. With this special man negotiation will no longer be dangerous or frightening.

Until then the daughter tries to act modestly to avoid being considered a bad girl, one who is familiar with off-color jokes and sexual innuendo, provoking danger and possibly her own undoing. The "bad" girl her mother has always held up to her is the author of her own fate, even if her fate is depressingly predictable: first, sexual promiscuity, then a bad reputation, then out-of-wedlock pregnancy, and finally, a miserable life with the callous and selfish father of the child or abandonment. The picture of the Bad Girl that the Mother has offered is frightening in its inexorable certainty that sexual autonomy leads to despair and no end of trouble.

Yet the daughter is fascinated by the bad girls she has seen because they are her first, perhaps only, symbols of rebellion from the rigid and constricting demands of femininity. Badness fascinates the daughter who has been forced to censor herself and be good for such a terribly long time. It is impossible not to envy the girls who seem to carelessly flout the rules of good-girl femininity: wearing obviously sexy clothes, talking back to parents and teachers, and being dangerously provocative with boys. The Bad Girl seems so tough, confident, and self-possessed as she swaggers down the hall, grinds out her cigarette in the office lunchroom, or sits comfortably at the neighborhood bar, alone and with authority. She seems invulnerable, but a little masculine. The Good Girl wonders if she is made of different stuff, but to assuage her jealousy she looks away and silently agrees with her mother that girls like that meet bad ends.

The Good Girl avoids trouble when she adheres to the requirements of femininity and enjoys being a girl. She must not call attention to herself since that could be misunderstood as demanding or aggressive. She learns to handle men by averting her eyes, changing the topic, acting like a buddy. She knows when to look offended, perplexed, indifferent, or outraged by men's conversational gambits. She knows her laughter is treasured as a sign of her interest, but she must not choose the wrong time to laugh, since she is supposed to take what men say seriously, as if she understood all their implications. If she learns to be modest and to defer to men in a variety of heterosexual encounters, she can control the forces of potential chaos that seem to engulf her when men approach.

She uses these socially supported techniques to feel in better control of the dangerous potential of sexual familiarity and her own sexual interest. As she fears men's opinions of her, she fears her desires to take them up on their innuendos and advances. Her indifference and disgust are often feigned to ensure her protection—if they believe she is without desire, men won't get the wrong idea about her goodness. While she is encouraged to say no to men and to refuse their advances, the daughter receives no encouragement to say yes, even though she often desperately wants to give up responsibility for being a humorless sexual monitor.

The social mandate to be good and refuse to show men the sexual side of her personality conflicts with her internal wish to be found attractive by men. The daughter desires to be thought of as good, but she wants men to look at her, to approve of what they see, to tell her in subtle and overt ways that she is a real woman. The winks, the stares, the whistles, even the obscene gestures, prove she is not invisible. She is still in the running with other women to get a man; she has what it takes, what they like. Gratefully, she walks by them, silently thanking each one for his appreciation. The fear of not being chosen is calmed. While she may turn indignantly from them, berating their crudeness and lack of respect, she enjoys these harmless and titillating forms of applause. This is the stage she occupies as she enters the gendered world of male and female. Her body stands for her femininity and her difference from men. Secretly she fills with the new power her body has given her. She can get men's attention. She has sexual power.

From this moment on, it is more and more difficult for the daughter to deny that her femininity is half the equation that is supposed to be completed when she joins with a man. From the time she realizes that her body is the undeniable symbol of her difference and her power, she accepts herself as a woman— a potential sexual partner to men. She must operate according to the rules and rituals of heterosexuality to have her unique traits as an individual appreciated and understood. She enters the arena of heterosexuality physically defenseless, socially powerless, but erotically powerful. She can't help but notice that her body causes disturbances in men. While this both pleases and frightens her, she understands that her body promises to end her invisibility, lift the veil, and bring her heterosexual happiness.

As the daughter secretly and guiltily cherishes her only source of power, the rules for feminine passivity require her to pretend that her body is not hers to use for pleasure. She must not act as a sexual author, entitled to pursue her own gratification, but cheerfully cultivate a demeanor of innocence and righteous indifference while she buries her active interest in the possibilities of the flesh. Free of responsibility in any potentially sexual situation, she shows others that she is "good."

The cultural ideology about the sexual nature of each gender allows the daughter to blame men for her sexual reticence. This ideology defines men as "naturally" aggressive and preoccupied with sexual gratification and women as "naturally" passive and only remotely interested in sexual fulfillment. The Victorian notion of men as predatory "beasts" whose arousal to sex brooks no interference serves to bolster women's investment in denying their own aggressive sexual longings. The pernicious effect of this division of the world of desire into active/masculine and passive/feminine encourages women in a magical belief that their very presence can incite men to acts of uncontrollable lust, which will ultimately harm women. The dangerous sensations the daughter experiences when her own murmurings of sexual interests intrude, in spite of her attempts to ignore them, can be conveniently placed on men, projected away from herself. Her own desires arouse such anxiety that the daughter expects to be punished for such feelings by those who will judge her as bad, namely, men, the gender that is not fooled by phony protestations of goodness.

No matter how convincing her passive stance, she worries that men will know what she is thinking. Therefore, she renounces the possibility of autonomy, to which she didn't feel entitled anyway, and decides to follow a proven formula for success. She dreams of finding a good man, postponing her sexual desires, and acting to ensure herself of men's good will and respect.

As she waits to be discovered, the obsession of heterosexual hope, of finding and being found by an exciting but safe man, carries her through her daily routine. She reserves a place for him in her heart. She wants a man who will tell her she is beautiful, clever, lively, warm, lovable. She needs a man who will tell her who she is and who she might become: someone to cherish her refined ability to nurture and support. Yet the daughter is not sure she will recognize her special man because so many men are manipulators and only interested in one thing. She hopes he will be honest, not trick or confuse her, con her out of her only defense in the world, her innocence and helplessness. Wondering if he will honor her fragility, praise her selflessness, and respect her lack of sexual sophistication, she stands before the stranger hoping he is not an opportunist.

The good man who will do for her and the bad man who will do to her live as strangers to each other in the daughter's imagination. The stranger may start out as a lover but with careful nurturance will soon take on the responsibility of caring for her in ways she has longed for ever since her disappointments in the family. The daughter dreams of her man, wonders if he will be as she imagines him, and searches for him in every man she meets. On the other side of heterosexual romance, on the darker side of her dreams of rescue and repair, lurks the rapist, a shadowy figure without a name or a face or a social identity. Unlike the husband, this stranger of mythic Evil stands outside the confines of the family, ready to punish daughters who step out of line. The threat of his attack is always present.

The daughter often thinks of the horror of the rapist's assault and what she must do to avoid him. If she doesn't keep a low profile, if she is too cocky, he might walk out of the shadows and punish her; if she returns a stranger's provocative glance, she is never sure he will not demand her to face death; if she radiates her sexuality and shows interest in the stranger who could be a future lover or husband, she may have to pay for her flirtation with an assault on her body or even her life. He is the culture's avenger for the daughter's attempt to have sexual autonomy without her mother's approval, without male protection and without fear. The setup is particularly unfair because the only way to feel good about herself, to affirm her femininity, is to attract a man who acknowledges her sexuality and finds her desirable.

In the culture's mythology, the rapist is a folk devil who lies in wait for innocent and unsuspecting virgins, who appears suddenly, without warning, to extract his payment of submission merely for the cruel and evil pleasure of reducing this feminine symbol of purity to a state of defilement and helplessness. The reality is no less brutal but the circumstances are certainly more banal. Many rapes merely extend traditional heterosexual exchanges, in which masculine pursuit and feminine reticence are familiar and formalized. Although rape is a gross exaggeration of gender power, it contains the rules and rituals of heterosexual encounter, seduction, and conquest.

At first the daughter notices a man looking at her, staring at her with some interest. She is not sure she wants to flirt with him or what his glance really means. If she decides right off that this man is dangerous or she is not in the mood to be playful, she ignores his insistent look, pretending she understands nothing of the sexual texture of his attempts to make contact.

But he seems to be interested in her and she is flattered and a bit excited by his attention. She finds him attractive too, but she is ambivalent. He pushes ahead, asking to speak to her, politely inquiring about her interests, her hobbies, and her availability. Poised between her fears of strange men and her desire for a romantic adventure, the daughter listens carefully to the coded language he speaks. Is she interested? Is he safe? Will she have sex with him? Will he kill her?

She is alert for suspicious signs, trying to verify her trust or sense of danger. Is she merely frightened because his attention makes her feel out of control? Are her feelings sexual or is she afraid? The daughter is unsure of the reactions in her body and the thoughts racing through her mind. More familiar with waiting to be chosen, the daughter hopes that if she has to surrender it will be because she wants to, not because she must. She consents to talk with him. She needs more information but at the same time monitors her behavior to show she is circumspect and respectable.

Used to having men take the lead in ordinary heterosexual encounters, she answers politely and asks him about himself. They laugh. He says how pretty she is. Is he telling her the truth or is it a ploy? She is afraid to cut off the conversation, afraid of angering him and provoking his masculine temper. She wants to please him by showing no sign of wariness or distrust. She counts on his good will to keep things friendly but not insistent. Speaking indirectly, afraid to say that she feels uncomfortable or is not interested in continuing their conversation, she changes the topic, smiles a lot, talks about subjects that present her as someone he might like, even sympathize with. She stalls for time and hopes to decide what she wants from their encounter. Although she fears misjudging this man, accusing him unjustly in her mind, she backs off from his questions and suggestions that she spend some time with him. Confused by the situation, unsure she has been able to read it correctly, she is bound by her niceness and her ambivalence to remain mute. She wants to give him, as she gives everybody, the benefit of the doubt. She hopes he will not transform himself from Dr. Jekyl into Mr. Hyde and exploit her defenselessness, forcing her to submit to violence and sexual acts meant to hurt and humiliate her. She hopes she is wrong about him. She prefers to believe he just wants to get to know her. How can she be so rude to him? Having been cautioned by women older and more experienced than she, the daughter is afraid to hurt his feelings, insult his masculinity, or appear suspicious, full of rape fears and fantasies—or sexually repressed. She doesn't want to run the risk of "turning him off" or "turning him on."

One woman, Harriet, recalls what happened to her when she was raped at 17:

> I often went to the movies alone, they were my only adolescent passion and none of the kids I hung out with were interested in what I saw as culture with a capital C. Although my parents were very strict with me and didn't allow me to date boys, wear makeup or hang out after

school, they never forbade me to travel alone into the city to see a movie.

That night there was a handsome young student ahead of me in the line and he started talking about this and that and asked if he could sit next to me. I was very flattered by his interest and since he seemed nice enough I said o.k.

We held hands in the movie and after, he asked me back to his place for a drink. I thought it was so sophisticated, just like in the movies. As we walked he said he thought I was very attractive. No one had ever said that to me before. In my family I was considered quite plain and I never thought of myself as pretty. My mother told me that smart girls shouldn't worry about being pretty.

I was ambivalent about going with him but I was also excited. I was surprised that as soon as we entered his apartment he locked the door, ordered me to strip and then sodomized me. I couldn't speak, could not say a word. I think I was in shock. My throat closed as if it would never open again. He sodomized me repeatedly and then told me to get out.

Vikki was also raped in adolescence, in a foreign country by a man introduced to her by a friend.

From the moment I saw Giovanni I thought he was the handsomest man I had ever met. He was a friend of a friend so I felt safe. When he asked me to come to his place for a drink I was ambivalent because I thought that in a Latin culture this might be taken as a sign that I wanted to sleep with him. And I would have perhaps at a later time but not at first. I wanted to get to know him, talk about his art and find out what he was about.

He did act very seductive toward me but it was very playful and not at all aggressive until I made a move to end the evening. As I was getting on my coat, he gripped my shoulders with force and said "You are not going to leave until I get what I want."

I pushed him away but he threw me on the floor and literally dragged me to the bedroom. He kept muttering about what he would do to me, brand me or shave my head or kill me and I was terrified. He looked like a madman, and had completely changed. For the next three hours he forced me to go down on him, while he ranted on about how he would have to tell the world about my shame. He said if I tried to leave he would have to kill me.

Tanya speaks about the man who raped her one night when she was walking home alone from the bus.

I wasn't afraid of him in the beginning. I know how to handle guys. They like to rap and I am usually friendly but firm. We had seen each other on the bus and shot friendly glances, nothing sexy, just that look when you check out the other passengers. He got off at the same stop as I did and started to walk behind me. I really hate that. Then he caught up with me and offered a cigarette, which seemed cool. He asked about my job, whether I liked cats, if I was into a spiritual trip, and what I was doing out so late. He was very polite so I trusted him. Then he asked me if I wanted him to come to my place and give me a massage. I laughed and said no thanks, but started to get nervous. Then all of a sudden he grabbed me, threw me on the ground and said, "If you don't let me fuck you I am going to kill you."

Meeting strange men, men unfamiliar and new, promises romance but simultaneously presents the threat of rape. It is no wonder that the daughter who is raped while "meeting a man" does not know whether she has the right to call the act rape and name herself a victim.

The daughter is familiar with being a sexual object because she has been encouraged to leave all sexual negotiations up to men, posing as a good girl and a feminine woman. When she was told to feign disinterest in things sexual, she was promised that men would take responsibility for the approach and the subsequent mechanics of seduction and its consequences. Her vulnerability assures men she is worth protecting, that she is pure in a modern sense.

Responsible only for making sure she is chosen, the daughter feels betrayed by the man who transgresses the heterosexual contract of romance, leaving her to face the devastating results of her feminine stance. Her defenselessness, which symbolizes her need for male protection, ensures nothing; it has served as provocation for violation and a temptation for acts of defilement. Defeated and humiliated through rape, the daughter's worst fears about men are validated. The battle of the sexes is no mere metaphor. She could have predicted her defeat. Although she was conditioned in daughterhood to be a victim, she refused to believe "it" would happen to her.

The daughter who is raped, living away from home, on her own and alone, without her mother, must come to terms with the meaning of her violation and the possibilities for future relations with men. She faces a complex and painful dilemma: She must integrate rape into her life and continue to look for a man who will care for her. She has to distinguish good men from those who will harm her, to take fewer chances and accept the feminine world view that men will take advantage of her if they can. From then on she will do anything to be in control, forced by circumstances to follow the mandate for good-girl behavior, which has been so oppressive but, like a self-fulfilling prophecy, so true.

The daughter who survives rape reports her experience with an initial calm that is unsettling to the listener. Her voice is reserved, almost distant, as if she is speaking about an event that is impossible to comprehend fully. She assures her listener that she is not full of rage or self-pity. She speaks of endurance in the face of invasion and the terror of losing control. She accepts her defeat as inevitable. She is resolved to endure and go on with her life. She appears to have exhausted her resources for understanding why rape happened to *her* and would like to forget the unanswerable questions.

Although she could not resist the attack, she takes solace in the fact that she refused to bow to his need for her to enjoy her violation. By cutting off all connection with her body, by escaping into her head, by not letting him kiss her as he raped her, she refused his attempt to define this terrifying act as just another sexual encounter. Because she could not defend herself from this random, vicious, and gratuitous act of violence, she claims one small victory by taking pride in her ability to endure.

Her endurance elevates her to the status of martyr in the battle of the sexes, and she is often transformed by rape into one of society's symbols of oppression. Through her experience she is added to the symbolic sorority of female martyrs, secular and spiritual, who represent purity defiled and sacrifice submitted to. Ironically, once she has been raped, she is seen as the quintessential symbol of defeated virtue, cherished as an icon of femininity by the same society that enforces the definition of her essence as purity and helplessness. She accepts her defeat as inevitable, one more act of surrender, the last station on the cross of femininity.

While society comforts rape victims with the mantle of moral superiority, it is a poor cover for people's ambivalent reactions toward victims of violence, especially when the assault is in broad outline so similar to normative heterosexual encounters. Although the culture reveres her for surviving male sexual aggression, it always suspects that she may have drawn disaster to herself. Society is prepared to blame the victim through its belief that only provocation causes men to violate the heterosexual contract to protect women. Helpless and passive victims seem to deserve more compassion, and in rape social definitions of appropriate feminine response to adversity are praised. Her shame is proof of her innocence.

While society is ambivalent about the moral standing of the victim, the daughter who is the object of sexual coercion tries to protect those she cherishes most from the frightening and confusing implications of rape. She is acting on her Good Girl script when she joins with them in denying the full impact of the event on her life, and in the conspiracy of silence, assuring them that she is really fine, that she can take her violation in stride and resume her life as if nothing had happened.

> I felt very guilty about what happened to me and for years I told no one, not even my mother. Now I realize I denied myself a lot of support but I was obsessed with the idea that I had let this happen . . . if I hadn't let him talk to

me, if I hadn't found him initially pleasant, if I hadn't spoken, then it would never have happened. Why wasn't I more suspicious? What happened to my instincts?

I never thought of telling my mother. We didn't have that kind of relationship, the one that so often is shown in ladies' magazines, where the mother is the girl's confidante. I must have thought she would have blamed me; after all, girls are responsible for all the bad things that happen to them and if it involves sex, it surely must have been my fault for being there in the first place.

She knows they are uncomfortable talking about the rape, that they are full of unformed questions and half-baked theories. She thinks she can protect them from feeling the rage and the horror, but she also worries that they might consider her hysterical if she dwells on her experience too long or with too much feeling.

Often embarrassed by her equanimity and lack of anger or despair, she wants to get back to her life, to sidestep the concern and pity of others. If she can gain control of her life, she will forget the terrible day; it will drop out of the calendar and fall into the past. She never wants to re-experience the feeling of being invaded, the loss of control, and the humiliation of being made into a strange man's victim. Heterosexuality is a more problematic arena than ever, yet returning to it feels imperative. She is determined to prove to herself and those who watch her that she will not generalize about gender relations; she will not become a man-hater.

As one woman recalls:

I felt numb, dead. Something had stopped working. In the space of a year I met a man who was very shy, not at all sexually like the men I had been attracted to. We married. I wanted desperately to get close to a man and prove to myself that I could be loved and treated well. I felt I needed a man who would accept me now that I had been "damaged." The marriage was cheered on by my mother but didn't work out. Now I wonder if I should have tried to marry so soon after the rape. I think I was doing penance for being attracted to the man who eventually raped me, and thought it wasn't right to have sexual pleasure after that. Also, the marriage proved to others that I was an innocent victim. I would piously refer to my victim status in order to exonerate myself from guilt.

Men, whom she formerly saw as her salvation and reward for being a good girl, became suspect—potential violators. By separating the rapist from other men and her feelings of betrayal from her hopes for future happiness, she tries to make peace with being a sexual victim.

Rape touches the old pains of daughterhood where rage and fury are locked away, muffled and distorted by repeated admonitions to accept whatever is meted out to her. She does not rage or curse or scream that she would like to kill her victimizers because she represses her anger and becomes an angel of mercy and compassion. Her reactions are feminine; she is used to turning the other cheek and muting her rage. She has forgotten how to tell the truth, even to herself, about the depth of her resignation to women's fate. She hesitates to state needs or claim from others the time and attention that might make her feel better. She denies her pain and depression to make life easier for those around her, returns to everyday life, grateful she wasn't maimed, but guilty for causing other people so much trouble. She says she is lucky, really lucky, to have gotten off easy—without being killed—reassuring herself and others of the prime importance of her survival.

Rape is a grotesque parody of heterosexual seduction that mocks the romantic image of heterosexuality and inviolable female purity. Through rape the daughter's social and sexual position is writ large. With blinding clarity, masculine power and feminine powerlessness assume their crudest and most literal forms, reducing the genders to the social roles of victim and victimizer. Thus, rape simultaneously violates femininity, validates the gender hierarchy, and teaches women that the limits of autonomy are narrow and dangerous. The paradox of femininity forces women to live with the contradiction of their love for men and their helplessness before them. It is therefore not surprising that women often choose to misunderstand the significance of rape and the ways in which they have been set up to be its victims.

Rape confirms the message the daughter receives in the nuclear family; the outside world is dangerous and men will either love her or hurt her; there is no way she can protect herself except by saying no to their demands. The daughter's fears about male sexuality, the aggressive mix of passion and violence, are realized when ordinary heterosexual encounters are transformed into rape. The stereotypic stance of femininity requires her to give up control over potentially sexual situations as she waits for men to make the first move. Rape is thus embedded in the context of "normal" heterosexual events. Longing for a man's attention, but afraid to control or take responsibility for the outcome of sexual negotiation, the daughter prepares during her apprenticeship in femininity to await masculine initiatives instead of taking control and making her desires known. Even if she desires to be left alone.

Rage is a betrayal of the daughter's trust in men's claims to protect her and see her for who she really is. In rape she is reduced to a faceless representative of her gender group, without a self, without a personality. Merely a symbol, a hole, a field of purity that tempts violation and encourages defilement. Her individuality is denied and brutally mocked, as the man who rapes her chooses her not for his lover but for his victim.

Rape reinforces the conditions of femininity because the daughter is again made to understand that she cannot control her life or her life chances. Autonomy and risk taking, ambivalently regarded before rape, are experienced by the rape victim as the inevitable road to disaster, defeat, and humiliation. Standing up for herself or protecting her own interests seems to be a futile exercise in a world where women are inevitably the victims of men. If her resources for resistance and self-definition were not totally depleted or defused as she grew up in the nuclear family, rape will surely teach her that strength and arrogance are not tolerated in women. Rape weakens the resolve of the daughter to make her own way and be visible in the world. She is refeminized through rape.

After being raped, the daughter wonders if her body, the object of men's attention and the source of their interest in her, betrayed her. She wonders whether it sent a message she could not control. Although she was groomed to use her body as a means of attracting men, she now fears that her body draws danger to her. The body that represents her vulnerability before men no longer feels like it belongs to her. She feels polluted and stigmatized in her very flesh.

The daughter's search for a good man after her victimization in the gender war is often desperate and fraught with feelings of guilt. Can a man accept a woman who has been defiled and dirtied by rape? Feeling like a loser, a victim, the daughter decides to suppress her sexuality and hopes to find a man who will accept her and understand. A good man will make her feel safe again.

7
LOVE AND DEATH: BATTERED WOMEN

The question most frequently asked in discussions of the social phenomenon of woman battering is, "Why do those women stay with the men who beat them?" The questioners often use an incredulous and somewhat disapproving tone of voice, the assumption being that there must be something wrong with *those* women. People rarely ask first, "Why do those men want to hurt their women?" Somehow, we find it easier to understand the frustrations and impulses that lead a man to strike out against a woman. As with a father striking a child, there could be many valid reasons: for his or her own good, to teach a lesson, to set needed limits, to punish, to make an impression. There are also less valid but perfectly understandable reasons: to vent frustrations, because the man's temper got the better of him, because the woman provokes him, because she needs it, because his subculture requires him to show love in this way. Men, so the cultural myth goes, lead lives of hard work, harsh competition, and struggle. It's no wonder they need to blow off some steam at home. They have to take what their bosses hand out to bring food to the table, so it's easy to forgive when they spread some of their hurt and anger around and take it out on mates or partners.

Many social thinkers whose perspective is essentially materialist, who see the major social problem as one of unequal distribution of the means of production, argue that this steam valve for men is the sad but inevitable outcome of an oppressive capitalist system, that alienation on the job turns men into machines and deadens their sensibilities, thus turning them against their own interests, even their own families. This view makes sense, on one level, but it omits the psychodynamics that "make the women stay." Neither does it explain the factors that lead one alienated, frustrated, oppressed man to beat his wife and another to work out in a neighborhood gym. What actually has to be explained is how women are molded into tolerant future victims of violence, and how men acquire the social control that enables them to violate their partners with impunity.

As mothers, we are both the victims and the origins of men's anger. We are often blamed for causing our children's anger, told that we are at fault for our children's aggressive feelings. We have to frustrate our children, to some extent, to aid in their struggle to grow. That kind of frustration—limits set to guide development or to ensure physical safety—is painful, but is usually far outweighed by the amount of real nurturance we can provide for our children. Children don't stay angry over that kind of frustration for long. Partly, social conditions require us to set limits on our children's expectations, on their freedom of expression, on their exploration of ideas—limits we consider essential to their safety. Because the same limits were set for us, we have no way of stretching them for ourselves. We find ourselves frustrating our children with our own limits, needs, worries, and unconscious strivings.

Nobody can be a good mother (a "facilitating environment") very long without a proper balance of rest, rehabilitation, and refueling. Infants need symbiotic relationships with their mothers. As psychoanalysts describe it, infants need to see their feelings validated in their mothers' eyes. Mothers have to suppress their stream of feeling and experience to provide "adequate mothering" for young children. Mothers who spend too much time in distress or depression while feeding young children mirror confusing information to them. Mothers who are just tired after a long day of careful nurturing may mirror lack of affect and interest in their children. It is difficult, if not impossible, for one person to provide adequate mothering. Even the best nurturer must be part of a family structure that allows for several (more than two) adults to rotate child care among them, leaving enough time for each to pursue personal interests while developing a continuous and intimate relationship with the child.

Most of us live in an environment in which mothering depends solely on an individual mother, a tired, harassed, oppressed, frustrated woman, who nurtures when she can, but who, in the end, sets limits that hurt daily and sharply. Mothers cannot help depriving children of needed attention, love, resources, and security. We simply don't have the requisite amount to give. We usually compound the damage by venting our own unhappy guilt for failure at mothering on our own deprived children. It's unfair to them, but we can't help it. When children get angry we may root for them inside, because anger is entirely appropriate as a response to deprivation and frustration. But it is hard to be the object of that anger.

Mothers treat sons differently from daughters when those sons express that anger. An angry little girl strikes us as unseemly. Her anger should never be more than a flash of intense emotion, followed either by tears or a demure apology. Overtly angry children are not sweet, and little girls are supposed to be sweet. We teach our daughters to suppress their anger. Starting with how we mirror it back: encouragement or assuagement. An angry little boy is charming, his anger spunky. His prolonged anger shows he has staying power. We try to teach him to channel his anger, not suppress it. We mirror back his anger encouragingly: "That's right, little fellow. You go ahead and yell your lungs out!" We teach him to delay gratification, to plan his strategy, to initiate action, to compete for what he wants, to cope with the world, to use his anger on his own behalf. Most of us succeed only partially in helping our sons channel their anger constructively, but we don't feel nearly so much like failed mothers for having angry young men for sons as for having "produced" bitter, angry, dissatisfied young women.

We not only actively try to "produce normal children," which means sweet girls and spunky boys, but we also feel differently about sons and daughters. Daughters remind us of ourselves. We frequently see ourselves in our daughters and reexperience, triggered by the reflections in our daughters' eyes, identical childhood feelings. Memories of childhood pain and rage throw us off. Suppressing our own emotions to care for a young child is hard enough, but when feelings that must be coped with instantly form strong, sharp, overwhelming memories of pain, deprivation, forbidden anger, frustration, rage, and yearning, the mixture becomes very explosive. At the very least, we don't want to *be* with our daughters when they trigger such emotions. We derive little pleasure in such interactions, which evoke only duty, depression, and possibly rage. We walk around clenched, tight, permitting no spontaneous or sudden change, stomping out all fledgling feelings. When we finally succeed in clamping down on our free-floating anxiety, we mope around, feeling like a partially deflated punching bag filled with beads of lead rather than beans. Or we may cry. Our children have no choice but to internalize such moods. Whatever spontaneous, lively, but potentially disruptive feelings we don't squash in them directly, they learn to stamp out by themselves. They learn that those feelings are no good.

Boy children trigger feelings too, of course, and we identify with them. But not as often, as painfully, or as treacherously. We are more confused about differences between our daughters and ourselves, less sure where one starts and the other leaves off. We expect the two-way mirroring to occur more easily. Boys, even after moments of intense identification, remind us more often of their difference. Boys need to assert their masculinity, their necessary difference from us, their struggle toward independence. So they remind us that they are different, not female, future men, after all.

Many mothers have mixed feelings about this fact. Girls remind us of ourselves and of our mothers, causing mixed feelings too. We have great expectations of making our daughters into better women than we were allowed to become and we also resent them for having a better life than we did. We tend to oppress daughters with endless stories of suffering at the hands of our mothers, thus reinforcing the tradition of enmity between women. It's normal for a daughter to hate her mother; it's how she's supposed to feel.

But boys! Boys are potential men. Many of us realize with shock, over and over again, that the sweet little boys before us will someday be men who will possibly oppress women, that the princes we're raising will automatically receive a number of women's best nurturing efforts for the rest of their lives. We raise our daughters to care for our sons in our stead.

And what has the prince ever done that we didn't do as well? What makes him so special? He is a male. He will one day be a man. He may be a good man, a savior, a protector, the good father we didn't have, the one who will be around when we need him. In that sense, we want him to grow up well and strong, and as fully as possible. Of course, once he actually becomes a man, we may find ourselves contending with a man who has little use for women, who may dislike us, and who will certainly feel superior to us.

Mothers feel about male children as we do about men in general, having been programmed by a similar system of myths, assumptions, perceptions, and commandments. We run the gamut from seeing men as beasts and babies to seeing them as knights and gods. Which of those feelings predominate, and their particular mix, is largely determined by individual histories and circumstances, but we are all playing in the same ball park. We give our sons more latitude, limiting them less, frustrating them too, but allowing them to channel their rage. We deprive our daughters more and then teach them that they must not respond in ways that are not nice.

So children grow up angry at mothers from a very early age. We punish them for their anger, take revenge on them for our suppressed anger at our own mothers, and let them know that they mustn't hate us for it, that our love, the stuff they need to survive emotionally, is entirely dependent on the successful suppression of their anger at us. So we frustrate and oppress our children, but we also nurture them. When our children love us, it is at least as much because the culture has forbidden them to hate us as because we have nurtured them.

Nurturers have been severely devalued. Mothering is supposed to be natural, something that comes easily, like breathing, that takes no skill or energy. There's something wrong with a woman who fails at mothering. Even animals can mother. A woman who can't, then, is less than human. A woman who can't do it properly (and secretly even the most mother-loving of us knows that our mother was not all that wonderful at it), is not a real woman at all, but a fraud. But even if she *can* do it, she isn't much. Anything women do is devalued, simply by virtue of being designated as a "feminine" activity.

Most of us grow up in nuclear families, or in shells of nuclear families (with phantom or absent parents), in which the mother has an inferior role by definition. If she doesn't, we certainly don't grow up proud and glad to tell the world about it. A domineering mother—and most nonsubservient women are called domineering to some degree—is a terrible and shameful thing for a child. "Domineering," as applied to women, is not so very far from the evil witches we all grew up with in childhood tales. Women who dominate are accused of turning boys into sissies and girls into hysterics. A child who has the misfortune of having a domineering mother is automatically tagged as having either a henpecked father (no real man would tolerate a domineering wife) or coming from a broken home or irregular family, which is immediately suspect. So if Mother is devalued, inferior, and plays out the myth or the reality that every major decision be left up to Father, boys are free to love her halo but despise womanhood, to canonize their image of her and thus defeminize her (Saints are beyond gender; they are divine) and hate women largely because women remind them of their mothers.

If Mother is devalued, girls are stuck with hating her, resenting her, and despising her, just as their brothers are. In addition, they have to prepare to become Mother (not to "get" her as boys will). A boy can grow up emulating his father, swearing to become a man like or absolutely unlike him, but he will certainly find a woman to take care of him (unless his mother has turned him "sissy," of course). Even his father found a woman to submit to him. So, if he thinks of his father as a positive example, he strives to become like him. If he sees his father as a negative example, he still gets reassurance from the fact that, even at his potential worst (just like his father), there will be a woman for him. He will despise that woman, of course, just as his father does his mother, but an inferior woman does not reflect badly on her husband. Great men often marry their secretaries because they make great wives. A woman who is forced to settle for an inferior (henpeckable) man is clearly perceived as a pathetic creature. Better than being an old maid maybe, but pathetic nonetheless. Girls are stuck emulating their mothers even though they rarely want to. If they want to, it is usually a sign that the cultural program has them completely in its sway. It is rarely in the interest of self-actualization that anyone wishes to become a martyr, a victim, and a loser. It just seems preferable to becoming a cold, domineering, unnatural bitch, which is how a girl is made to feel when she considers herself first. A girl wants power too, Father's power, but can get it only through or from him. She has to learn to please him, to hook him, as Mother did. She keeps trying to please him, even when he doesn't think much of her and treats her insensitively, even when she is not sure why she is being subservient anymore, but sure she is not getting the power she wants.

So women try to marry power. We marry men who seem to have it, who seem willing to share it or to use it to protect us. Men, as well as women, marry in an attempt to create and establish the symbiotic bond we needed and never achieved with our parents. We are finally going to have somebody who loves us to ourselves. Men marry women, by and large, whom they consider improvements on their mothers or who remind them of their mothers. Men marry good girls and then are furious because they are reminded of the good mothers who deprived them. A good girl is a rotten mother, of course, because she has to suppress more silently, more sneakily. She doesn't do well by her son's anger because she makes it necessary for him to be "good" around Mom. No rough language, no strong feelings. A good girl doesn't put out; she deprives her children of herself. A good girl certainly can't furnish the healing symbiosis we all want with our partners. No one could, of course, but we have nobody to blame but ourselves, our aging parents, our confused mates, and our deprived children. So we blame some or all of the above. There is no doubt that it *is* unfair, so we have to blame someone.

Women don't get to merge, or to have power, except for some reflected acceptance. We don't get the relationship with our fathers we yearned for, nor "adequate mothering" from our marriages. But every cultural message encourages us to keep hoping, to believe in romance, to yearn for that grand symbiotic union in love, in sex, in daily living, to look for the right person, or to work away at our marriages with techniques for "rekindling romance." We are disappointed and blame ourselves. Men are permitted a greater claim to their anger. When symbiosis fails in adult life, they get mad. Some men are more deeply and more consistently angry than others, but the nature of their anger is no different from other men's.

Batterers are not, as a group, recognizably different from the rest of the population. They batter women, vent their deeply felt rage on women, because they can get away with it. It's a version of kicking the dog or the furniture. Women would like to kick the dog too, but we have been taught to suppress that urge and nobody is available for us to kick except our children. It is far less satisfying to express anger on a helpless child than on a full-grown adult who won't hit back.

Men do it because nobody stops them. A man who beats up on his woman may be a little more brutish than we consider admirable, but he is not a freak or a monster, a psychopath, a drug addict, or an alcoholic. He may be considered crude, not fully civilized, but in a working-class man that may merely be considered the dark side of his male market value, and in a middle-class man a welcome sign of unrepressed virility. Anyhow, some women like it. . . .

It is unfeminine to be in touch with negative feelings. Women are not supposed to be aware of their aggression, rage, negativity, or nastiness. A woman who is too clearly aware of her negative feelings might be inclined to express them in an unfeminine way. A man who blows his top, loses his temper, or lets off some steam is just a man. A woman who has uncontrollable outbursts of rage, throws temper tantrums, or lets her anger out on the people around her is a sick person. She needs help; something is wrong with her. What is "wrong" with her, of course, is that she is in touch, at those moments, with her adult self, who is justifiably enraged at the same sources of distress and frustration any sane adult would rail at. She sees herself in a realistic relation to the world, as someone who is acted upon, who gets angry when treated unfairly. She can also act upon others, when she wants to, as in venting her rage. She is not a martyr or a saint. She is capable of accepting responsibility for her actions, for good or ill, and being independent.

A woman more deeply steeped in feminine ways, which includes accepting the double standard in all its forms, cannot take full responsibility for anything she does; she can take only the blame. The fact is that after an initial, unexpected assault (either verbal or physical), she either permits unequal expression of violence and rage in her relationships, or she fights against it and puts a stop to it. If her lover screams at her in rage whenever he has had a rough day, she may not really mind. A good yell can get things off her chest too, and then she feels better, better able to relax and actually engage with others. The trouble comes when the man has the right to yell and scream, but the woman doesn't, either because she doesn't feel she can do that, or knows she shouldn't want to, or he doesn't like it, and she lets those reasons stop her. Even when no violence is involved, at least no physical violence, or even strong, psychologically abusive language, accepting male rage and suppressing female rage, relatively speaking, is a setup for battering. Men, who are allowed their anger at failed symbiosis with their chosen partners, are more likely to express that anger. They are more apt to feel anger toward the women who can't always give them what they need. As women, we are much more likely to blame ourselves and be out of touch with or deny the anger we feel toward men when men fail to meet our need for symbiosis. When we accept men's need as being greater than our own, we collaborate in our own oppression.

Battering always occurs more than once. It becomes part of an intimate relationship. In many ways, it becomes the center of that relationship, even though women often talk about it as a rare, exceptional occurrence, a time when the angry man "is not being himself." If we view outbursts of bad temper as exceptional rather than occasional, we are also apt to interpret outbursts of violence as something different, not part of the actual fabric of our relationships. By denying that violence occurs regularly, if only occasionally, we are less prone to deal with it, to recognize it as a tremendously important and revealing occurrence that has to be dealt with thoroughly. It merely becomes a man's exaggerated temper tantrum, an explosion that means he was feeling a little worse than he did at other times. We deny it as a signal or an event.

We certainly don't discuss the problem with outsiders, or with insiders either. It is extremely dirty linen, even if we acknowledge its existence. It didn't really happen, or if it did, it wasn't the way it would sound if we heard someone else tell it, or it doesn't mean what it would mean if it happened to another woman.

"It doesn't mean anything..." We hide it so it *won't* mean anything. We know it would be significant in the world. Such things are not supposed to occur in loving relationships, and they don't, to regular people. Our oppression becomes our shameful secret. The need to control ourselves, never to let on, to keep the faith and the secret, lowers our already maligned and underdeveloped self-esteem. We know we would be considered inferior if we let on about our secret, and we're probably right. Battered women are suspect; they must like it, they must be sick. We realize the danger in being ourselves, which reinforces our sense of having something terribly wrong with us. We arrive at a false solution to the problem by denying its existence to the outside, and by trying to deny it to ourselves.

Rape is frequently a part of battering. Or the violence itself, the beating, is sexual in nature and content. Women are often accused of precipitating sexual crimes. If we wear attractive clothes or take a walk alone, we are "asking for it." So we make a connection that seems entirely natural; we recognize our own sexuality as evil. It is hard to be sexual and good at the same time. Feminine "sexuality" is supposed to be all-passive, all-waiting, all-alluring, and teasing and accepting. We are told we must practically die from the sheer power of the surrender.

An active woman who expresses her sexuality in also wanting, grabbing, demanding, insisting, and mastering is pornographic. Some men may find her desirable, although certainly not as a wife because she is not feminine. Female sexuality is supposed to be an empty vessel thirsting to be filled with male energy and power. We all know that men get blue balls, but we're supposed to blush at the very thought of desire, to see it as through a filter, transformed to a hazy glow of warmth, light, and fragrance. No panting, none but the most involuntary sounds. Women are permitted to let out an involuntary sigh of uncontrollable passion at surrender (orgasm), but we certainly shouldn't use erotic words, want to talk about sexual technique, or express ourselves during or prior to sex. Men fuck, women love and swoon. But we aren't like that. We suspect we have a more active sexual self somewhere inside, possibly infantile, possibly dirty, probably inappropriate, and certainly unknown. Whenever we experience anything of that active sexual energy (from flirting at the office to reading dirty books), we sense, whether we know it or not, a part of that positive, angry, aggressive self that wants to take responsibility and grow up strong, not feminine. We want to be ourselves, which we know is not right, not what we're supposed to be. So that aggressive, "not right" sexual self is the root of the problem, the evil core we try to hide.

We end up feeling bad about ourselves for that, of course. It's terrible to feel evil at the core, but it is also important. It's the way to explain what's wrong to ourselves, and thus to take control of the situation. We prefer the grandiose notion of an evil core to the pathetic recognition of our own arbitrary oppression. We prefer taking the blame to feeling like innocent and helpless cogs in the grand machine of patriarchal culture. We prefer being the bad one to being a mere vehicle for men's tantrums, a punching bag men use while they go about their business. Who wouldn't?

A woman who doesn't follow her impulses toward blame-taking is apt to feel even worse, helplessly caught up in a hostile net of someone else's anger, disappointment, and disapproval. She is likely to be permanently afraid. After all, if she causes an outbreak of violence, she can control it, at least negatively: She can make it happen, and, in a way, make it *not* happen. She can't really make it not happen, of course, but she can keep working on it, looking for the right formula, the right way to handle it. She feels that one day she will know how to control it. If the violence just comes out of nowhere, like a vicious flash of lightning from an indecipherable sky, she can't afford to feel anything but fear. She becomes immobilized. Anything can bring it on, at any time. Nothing is safe; nothing is much safer than anything else. It makes no sense. She becomes helpless and phobic, unable to move, to function outside her home (the center of the violence). She becomes confused and panicked, and does everything wrong, thus calling more anger on her head and confirming her worst suspicions about nothing being safe for any length of time.

So a battered woman uses the very violence she suffers as evidence for an explanatory principle: The fact that she can make that essentially sweet, reasonable, even timid man so mad that he beats her is incontrovertible proof that she is no good, hopeless, evil, and worthless. This, furthermore, explains what has always been wrong with her, why her parents treated her as they did, what they tried to tell her all along. She was never any good. She is a failure as a woman. Battering becomes understandable and forgivable. Although it is a rationalization, it seems to explain all that childhood loss, deprivation, exclusion, and pain.

A battered woman has little choice about feeling that way if her only other option is to feel like nothing at all. She's either at fault or barely present, meaningless, a mere receptable for men's rage and frustration. It has to do with the particular two-gender system we are stuck with. In our culture, the genders are antagonistic in a very unbalanced way. Each gender is *not* conceived of as a mix of positive and negative qualities, distributed differentially across women and men. Some apparently objective social thinkers would have us believe that women have some good qualities, like warmth and flexibility, and some bad ones, like vanity and irrationality, and that men have some good qualities, like strength and efficiency, and some bad ones, like pigheadedness and insensitivity. Together they make up a perfect human being, we are told, hence that irresistible urge toward heterosexual coupling. Actually, our gender system is very different. To be masculine means to have certain qualities, and to be feminine means not to have those qualities. One gender is the real thing, the other is second rate, degraded, devalued. Women shouldn't be any of the things men (people) are, or any of the things we are told to be either (see Chapter 1). Women are supposed to be all things to all men, and nothing at all. We are not supposed to possess any strength, but must endure indefinitely, yet stay delicately fragile (no hard skin as a result of scar formation, ever!). Women are supposed to be the absence of strength, to bend when men blow. So of course we permit the unequal expression of rage and collaborate and deny and forgive and forget and hope and pray. We are just doing what is supposed to come naturally.

Since we don't grow up feeling like equal partners in a fair gender system and thus gravitate naturally toward our other half, heterosexual coupling has to be legislated. Since a woman is nothing, she needs a man to make her into something. A man merely needs a woman to settle down. Two men together are friends, which is considered noble for men. Men have to be granted certain privileges to agree to expend any energy on their relationships with women. Men have to be bribed with sex and creature comforts. The male view makes sense: Why give up something for nothing, your friends for a bunch of girls? Women don't need incentives to form heterosexual relationships, which are their survival, their becoming, their being. A woman has to hook a man, to find him and keep him and please him and breathe some life into him by introducing him to the life of emotion. For all our pain, we get a chance to make him real. Our reward is being allowed to be, and making him as much of a real person as we can so we have someone to be with. In addition, heterosexuality is enforced through sanctions against anyone who does not practice it properly. Women who prefer partners of our own gender are considered sick, evil, criminal, and pathetic.

So the only option is heterosexuality or celibacy. A woman who practices heterosexuality outside the cultural tradition is considered a whore, a nymphomaniac, or a very sick woman. She must practice heterosexual celibacy until she's found a man to sanctify her body. A woman who practices celibacy outside the cultural tradition—in the home, the convent, or the old-age home—is a pathetic old maid, a failure, a joke. She must practice celibacy in prisons assigned to her by the patriarchy.

To prepare us for this compulsory heterosexuality, we must look forward to a life in which we play Cinderella, waiting for our sons to rescue us from the men we married to escape our fathers. We must believe. First, that the fathers who dominated our childhoods (whether in person or in absentia) really meant to protect us. Then we have to believe that the men we marry will love us even though they have been taught to dominate and despise us; we have to believe we are indispensable in men's lives. We have to believe that the sons we nurture will not grow into men who will hurt us. Finally, we must believe that each succeeding generation of men will protect us from themselves and each other. The better we have become at denial, at taking the blame, the better able we will be to believe any of this, over and over, even in the face of mounting evidence to the contrary.

An entire culture, one that is rich, complex, compelling, and profound, has been invented to create and reinforce those beliefs in women. The only difference—if there is any—between women who suffer being battered mercilessly by cruel, violent men and women in general is that the battered women have swallowed those beliefs more wholeheartedly and are held captive in their sway. A battered woman is more feminine. She often cannot remember anything about her childhood and talks as though her life was uneventful until she met and coupled with her man. She has a particularly hard time recognizing the competitive feelings she might have had toward her brothers, or the fear and rebellion she felt in relation to her father. She denies her past feelings of inequality and inferiority in relation to men and insists that she expected to start life all over with her present partner. We all do this to a certain degree, of course, but battered women tend to be particularly feminine.

The more feminine women are, the more we have been programmed for victimization. To be feminine means to be fragile, helpless, ineffectual, compliant, and distressed, as well as enduring, modest, altruistic, emotional, and cooperative. What more could one ask from a potential victim, except that she be willing to suffer, able to be a victim, unable to stop being one, willing to forgive her victimizer, and ready to take it again?

Abuse, both in childhood and in adult life, makes it more difficult to change that program for victimization to something safer and more functional, because violation refeminizes us. We have been taught to endure and suppress. Good girls endure their pain and suppress their rage. If we don't endure and suppress, we are blamed and punished for not being quite good enough. Apparently we haven't endured enough, or silently enough, suppressed only partially, not been totally gracious and warm in the face of frustration, humiliation, and stress.

A battered woman must have provoked abuse, otherwise it wouldn't be happening: Someone who is supposed to love her is so angry that he wants to kill her, or at least harm her. She tries to be even better. She tries to prevent further punishment by enduring more silently, by smiling more often, forgiving more easily. She experiences each further violation as more proof of her failure to be a good girl. So she tries harder and harder to less and less avail. And, of course, whatever spunk and self-esteem, however rudimentary, she began with gets literally beaten out of her. She ends up more afraid that things can go wrong, bring on a beating, cause a disturbance. She becomes more immobilized, depressed, and less able and less likely to do anything to help herself out of her predicament. Lenore Walker called it "learned helplessness." It is progressive, widespread, and often fatal. A battered woman also believes more strongly in the myths even though they have all been turned on their heads. The promise of male protection has turned into the reality of male violation. Everything she needs and hopes for has been threatened, so she holds on tighter, believes harder, denies more, to make her head stop spinning.

So when we find ourselves battered, which all women could (there is no way to tell the batterers from the rest of the world),

our survival depends on our responses. Most battered women
respond to abuse in particularly feminine ways. All women are
supposed to be soft and bleed easily, to be in constant danger of
bleeding to death. We are in constant need of a man's protection. We are also supposed to be martyrs, to suffer our pain
gladly and to endure the unendurable. A real woman would let
herself be torn limb from limb for her loved ones. Yet the
woman who faces torture with spiritual fortitude when it means
serving those she loves is also supposed to swoon at the sight of
blood. The only way to resolve the contradiction is to swoon
with spiritual fortitude under torture, to graciously accept the
torture as inevitable if mysterious, never to fight back or even
protest. So when the battered woman begins to realize that her
husband is going to beat her, when he has that look, when his
rage seems clearly out of control, she is not supposed to defend
herself, walk out, grab a weapon, or call for help. She is supposed to hold her breath, grow faint with fear, and wait for the
pain she knows is coming and that she knows she has to endure.
"Mary" told this story:

> Don had been beating me at least once a month since
> our first child was born, five years ago. After the first few
> times, when I was so shocked I couldn't think straight, I
> could always tell when it was going to happen. Things
> would get very tense between us and everything I did
> would set him off into a rage. I would try to calm him
> down and smooth things over but it wouldn't work. I
> often thought of taking the children and leaving, but I
> really didn't know where to go and I thought he'd find
> me anyway. Finally he would start to scream at me and
> put me down. I knew that if I screamed back he would
> explode, beat me, and then the tension would be over for
> a while. I would bring on the beatings just so he would
> be nice to me the next day.

A battered woman, who has often survived chaos and terror
in her childhood as well, learns to become increasingly helpless,
so she can fight less and less. She becomes more and more dependent on her man, his approval, his good will, his permission,

his moods. Since anything she does could set him off, she does less and less, to prevent his explosion. (We all forget how to do things when we are in a panic or when we feel hopeless about our efficacy. The more terrified we are, the more we bungle, forget, and give up.) If all that matters is how a man feels and whether he will explode or not, his response becomes much more important than the ability to do anything. It doesn't matter whether she really knows how to do something, just whether he's satisfied. Since he never is for long, a battered woman does not know how to do anything right.

Ruth was married to a man who had battered her for fifteen years. She had left him four times, but each time he had tracked her down and persuaded her to come home. He continuously threatened to kill her or himself if she left, a threat Ruth believed he meant and was capable of carrying out. She felt frightened most of the time and had been hospitalized twice for injuries she sustained when her husband beat her. Although she had heard of a crisis hotline on the radio, she felt no one could really help her with her problems. She'd never be able to get away unless she committed suicide.

A woman is supposed to be altruistic and ineffectual, to do endlessly for others, but never accomplish her goals. She is supposed to be always in a tizzy, always scurrying, but always focused on her loved ones. When he gets so mad that he beats her, she is supposed to take the blame, to feel she's made another mistake in her endless series of mistakes, and to empathize with his rage and disappointment. She is supposed to take the rap, feel his pain and endure his beating in silence. A battered woman actually does empathize with his pain. She often says she can't leave him because he might be hurt, might be lost, might be upset, might even kill himself. She feels for him, not for herself. And she is often ready to take the blame.

Linda knew that John had a temper when she married him. She also knew that he was under a lot of pressure on his job. One evening he began shoving and punching her when she didn't have his dinner ready on time. She agreed that she was wrong to be such a bad wife, and has tried harder to please him since then. Although he has battered her many times since, she says she doesn't believe that he really wants to hurt her. She often lies to her family and friends about her bruises and black eyes, insisting that she gets them from being clumsy and having accidents.

A battered woman takes the rap because it is better than having no control at all (it's better to think the crisis is her fault, because then she might be able to do something about her situation). She focuses on his pain because she has been taught to focus on others, never herself. She doesn't even know how to focus on herself. When she tries to, she feels selfish and guilty and switches to thinking about her children, parents, husband, friends, bosses. She thinks about herself obliquely, only in comparison with others, and often with dislike. Being preoccupied with herself makes her vain and selfish: a failed woman.

Barbara always knew when Tom was going to beat her. For a few nights before the attack, he'd come home slightly drunk and pick a fight with her about anything she said. Then he'd act menacing and shout that she was a vile, disgusting creature who didn't deserve to sponge off him for the rest of her life. He'd threaten to throw her out of "his house." She would cry and plead and beg him to stop saying such bad things about her, but her tears only seemed to make him angrier. Finally, when she felt hysterical and crazy from his verbal attacks on her, she would scream that he should just beat her and get it over with because she couldn't stand it anymore.

Women are supposed to be timid and compliant, but filled with emotions, to wear our hearts on our sleeves, but do whatever we're told without a peep. So when we are threatened with violence, we are supposed to take it meekly, to submit fully, and to be totally in touch with all we feel (pain) but not cry out loud. Silent but profound tears of remorse and hurt and love are supposed to trickle down our cheeks, copiously but quietly. The remorseful woman takes her punishment gratefully, passion-

ately. A battered woman complies hysterically. She has been
taught to accept the beating and appeal to men's mercy through
her pain and anguish. No defense, no retaliation.

On the contrary, she is supposed to cooperate in her own
humiliation and denigration. She is supposed to vilify herself,
recognizing that she is the sinner who deserves what is coming
to her. Her salvation lies in the man's righteous forgiveness,
achieved through her punishment. A woman is expected to tear
her hair out while a man beats her to a pulp. No combat, nothing that takes even a second's worth of clear, goal-oriented
thought: "How do I get out of this situation?" A battered
woman often feels guilty for the thoughts of escape and rescue
she "indulges in."

> Lorna has been battered by her husband, Joe, over many
> years. She thinks it started when he began to believe she
> was seeing other men whom she met at her job. She tried
> to reassure him that there was no man but him in her life,
> but he said she was lying and hit her in the chest, knock-
> ing her to the floor. Since then there have been many phys-
> ical attacks in relation to Joe's jealousy and accusations of
> infidelity. She often thinks of leaving him at those times,
> but later feels sorry for him because he had such a rough
> time as a kid growing up in an orphanage. She also feels
> guilty about wanting to get away from him since he obvi-
> ously needs her so much. Anyway, the bruises heal pretty
> fast.

So there the battered woman stands: bleeding but enduring,
learning to be helpless, taking the blame for her victimization,
and feeling sorry for her torturer. She is compliant, hysterical, and
willing to cooperate in her own humiliation and abuse, all to
pretend it isn't true, didn't happen, and doesn't mean what she
thinks it does. A very feminine woman, prone to passive acceptance of victimization, stays mesmerized by this situation. To
become that feminine, that martyred, she was probably punished often (if only by her parents' withdrawal of love and approval) for not being a good enough girl. She is trying to be
very, very good. She is willing to die to prove how good she can

be. Nobody, not even a well-socialized woman, stays in such a situation for long unless something beyond the present relationship with her battering man holds her there. Unless she is deeply self-destructive, she must call on some sense of self-preservation to end the torture. She will end it unless the situation feels familiar, like the human condition for women who are not much good, or unless she keeps hoping that this man, this menace, is more tortured than cruel, that one day she might cure him, get him to love her and be the benign protector she always yearned for.

Looking for protection from a violently abusive man makes no sense unless a woman has come to believe, in childhood, that that's the way men are, or are supposed to be, and that she can't live without them. We must assume that what pulls a woman in the dangerous direction of a violent man is the old hope of symbiosis with our parents—first with our mothers, and later with our fathers. A battered woman plays out a scenario she understands as the given in heterosexual relations. She is repeating, in some form, what she learned in the family, and what was done in the name of love.

Emotional preoccupation with achieving a union in the past, regardless of the cost in present pain, blinds us to real danger in the present. Countless women are scarred or crippled by their husbands in "accidental" injuries they blame on themselves. A man who beats a woman once is extremely likely to do it again, and the more often he does it, the more the violence will escalate. Yet she remains mesmerized by this situation, filled with longing and yearning and unfulfilled wishes and dreams and needs because she is waiting for her idealized father.

When she no longer sees the man she married as protector from and against the past, many a battered woman realizes that she thinks of her man as an emotionally unstable little boy. The evidence is in the violence itself: He goes crazy, he goes off, he is not as in control of himself as he pretends to be, and he is obsessed with his own need to be obeyed as an absolute authority. The violent man's woman recognizes that her man wants a mother, and when he is not being mothered as he wishes, he freaks out. But after the "episode," he breaks down, begs the woman's forgiveness, and brings her flowers; he promises never to do it again, says he doesn't know what got into him, that he never wanted to hurt her, that he would die without her and kill himself if she left him. Such a man offers every image of romance her culture promised her.

And the woman believes it. She knows she is dealing with an unstable, mixed-up, little boy-man, but she chooses to believe what he says, to deny what she knows. For one thing, it is far too painful for her to recognize the enormity of the crime committed against her person. It is totally dehumanizing to realize that someone she loves, and who has promised to love her, has used her body as a piece of living flesh on which to vent his rage, that it never had anything at all to do with her, just with his need and her availability. For another thing, a battered woman has learned, more than most of us, to focus away from her own experience at all times. It makes denial easier, and it makes it possible for her to confuse the pain she experiences with empathy for his suffering. She is sincere when she consoles the remorseful batterer. She may have moments of unrecognized but threatening rage, but quickly turns them to pity. (For example, when we are extremely angry at a young child who has innocently and inadvertently hurt us—bitten a nipple, pulled hair, jabbed us in an eye—we are so ashamed of our automatic feelings of rage that we immediately cuddle and caress the child to cover up that moment of genuine hostility. It would be enough simply to disengage the child gently and change position; the child is not in pain, we are. But we don't feel free to express our hurt and anger except through inappropriate identification with the child.) Many times a battered woman recognizes her moments of pure rage when the violence starts only after a good deal of emotional work with professional help. She certainly doesn't know how to use it or act on it to defend herself. Instead, she turns it around and feels compassion and pity for the object of her rage, thus turning her rage against herself.

Then there is the aftermath and its charms. A feminine woman yearns for romance, her only hope because she can't do anything for herself. This yearning is so strong that romance seems worth any price, even death and destruction. He doesn't keep it up for very long, of course, and sometimes he stays mad for a long time before the fit passes. But romance, the emotional high after survived danger, the relief of its termination, is a fine thing to focus on, preferable to the pain of the battering. The beating recedes into the past, a mere occasion for emotional release, and the romance of making up becomes the goal of the future: "If I am a very, very good girl, he will always want to treat me like this."

It is common for a battered woman to believe that her man is himself only at those times of remorse and reconciliation. He has feelings, he cries, he is no longer behind the macho façade she fears. The mask is off and the soul of the poet emerges. This is the man she married, the man she loves. That other guy is some monster who appears when the man she knows gets upset, hurt, and confused, when life gets to be too much for him, or when she provokes him. She wishes she could control the monster who is the cross she has to bear in their marriage. And to some extent this is convincing: The man is only allowed to express softer, more feminine feelings at moments of great distress. He becomes more real, acts more like another woman. He sounds very much like her, begging and whining and crying and pleading. She could actually connect with this guy when he acts that way. She knows he is sincere when he says he's sorry; she can tell. His tears are real. So is his fear that she will abandon him. He wants her, and he wants his mommy too. She'll be nicer to him than his mommy was: she won't upset him anymore. They'll both try harder, together. This is the kind of open emotional communication she has been hoping for. After the crisis is over, and before the next one starts to build up, he is much more accessible, more preoccupied with being a regular guy. He would probably kill her if she ever let on to anyone that he occasionally puts his head in her lap and cries like a baby. Then she's back to being the little woman and he is the big man. So sometimes it seems worthwhile to put up with the beating, just to get some of that loving behavior afterward. We all say that: "Sometimes we don't mind fighting because making up is so much fun." Of course, in this case he does all the fighting.

It is also likely that, at the moment of remorse, when her man is on his knees begging forgiveness, begging her not to leave, promising the moon, clearly desperate, guilty, confused, and upset, the battered woman feels a moment of triumph, a moment of gender equality, which, like the experience of pure rage, might threaten her femininity. That moment of equality can send her scurrying back into the feminine role, forgiving all and offering herself as a better doormat to her batterer. Gender loss, loss of feminine identity, is worse than physical pain; for some it is worse than death. Gender loss means having no identity at all. He must be all man, and she must be all woman.

The particular viciousness of this cycle of forgiveness and abuse lies in the fact that every violation validates the battered woman's feminine identity and thus makes her more of what she thinks she wants to and ought to be. When she is suffering, miserable, in pain, serving the needs of others before her own, frightened and helpless, she is more "natural," more feminine, more what she has been taught to believe she should strive to become. Growing up into a woman means growing up into a victim. Being battered is congruent in some way, or at least not discrepant, with her expectations. Maybe she didn't expect to be hurt (men are there to protect women), but when hurt, she responds like a victim and martyr because she has been taught that's what women are like. This notion puts her into an absolutely untenable conflict, of course: Women are their most "natural" selves when they are most in pain. This terrible, soul-crushing conflict is real for most women, battered or not, to some degree. For battered women the pain is more physical, more complex, more devastating, more continuous.

Many times a battered woman goes back to her batterer even after she has tried to escape, after she has talked to crisis counselors and been offered asylum in a shelter or has found an alternative living arrangement. She often expresses the incredibly crushing sense of inevitability she experiences when she considers getting away from her torturer. She imbues her man with magical powers. She thinks the batterer can see her from miles away, reach her through walls, find her wherever she hides. (Since her man is not only her torturer but her hope for salvation, a battered woman also wishes him to have the magic and joins him in creating the impression that he is omnipotent.) The pressure of constant abuse, the loss of self and self-esteem, the pain and fear, have made her hopeless. She is depressed and debilitated and fears that her man represents danger, not magic. The ponderous weight of years of feminine socialization makes a battered woman feel there is no way out, that life will always be the same, that she carries the curse with her wherever she goes.

For anyone burdened with fatalism and steeped in despair, the intensity of the battering crisis is a kind of relieving excitement, a form of negative intensity. Sometimes, when we are severely depressed, pain is a welcome reminder that there is life left in us. Male anger is at least a response. In some parts of this culture we are taught to believe that a man "cares enough to beat her," that his violence is a sign of love. In this way too, violence validates identity: A real man beats up on a real woman out of passion. A good smack never hurt anybody, and sometimes a woman really wants it. It turns her on. What "turns her on," of course, is the moment of negative intensity and excitement that breaks through the interminable depression and hopelessness of a resigned, beaten, hated, second-class human being.

Many battered women are highly sophisticated, middle-class, educated, competent women who apparently function very well in the public world. Inside their marriages or intimate relationships, however, they are helpless. They act helpless even when they are not, having learned to be that way. Any sign of independence seems to make their men feel deprived or left out, even if they are successful at their work and hardly ever home. So such a woman hides her competence, stifles her talents, turns off her admirers. She collapses into a scared puddle at home. Her man knows, of course, that she is not really helpless; she holds a full-time job, brings up three children, and entertains his colleagues and friends all the while, like any other "super-woman." What provokes him, then, is both her ability to survive on her own, her less-than-total need of him, which makes him feel infantilized and threatened with castration, and her helplessness, which prevents her from being the strong, ever-available mother he yearns for. Beating the shit out of her (usually with accompanying deadly verbal assaults) makes him feel he's in control again, and that it serves her right for not taking proper care of him.

His outraged insistence that she be the fragile but safe bridge over troubled waters (his own feelings), the vulnerable but inexhaustible breast he feeds on, is entirely consistent with what she believes she should be. So, even as she suffers the consequences of her doomed inability to be the impossible, his enraged violation of her makes her feel more acceptable, more successful as a woman. She proves her love and femininity, for which he married her, after all, by being his willing victim. She accepts, as an inevitable and natural part of that feminine identity, that he despises her—as does the rest of the world—and that he has good reason. He hates her for the very qualities of a victim—weakness and passivity—she has been forced to accept as her only birthright.

8
AUTONOMY
Emerging from Daughterhood

At a certain point in adulthood, I realized that I wasn't giving myself enough nourishment. It's not that I wasn't eating, it's just that what I was eating was not above subsistence level. I was surviving day to day, getting by, even doing things in my life, but I wasn't feeling very well. I experienced my life as a chronic, low-grade infection from which I would probably never recover—or die. I felt doomed to going on in this way, always feeling ill.

I didn't really know how to give myself nourishment. I knew how to eat, in an odd, unconscious, compulsive way, but I didn't know how to select what I needed from what was available. I didn't know how to chew or digest. I certainly didn't know when to stop eating. I had been told to eat everything on my plate regardless of whether I liked or wanted it. Letting someone else fill my plate seemed so much easier than making choices, so much easier than tuning in to my own hunger.

I was also afraid of rejecting anything on the plate for fear of missing something good, going hungry later when supplies were no longer available (a constant threat), or of making a mistake and irrevocably rejecting a valuable possibility. In short, I had to trust in my ability to make a decision on my own behalf. I would never know when I was hungry, and even if I did, I would never be able to feed myself. I would not know when my hunger had been satisfied and so I would go on forever without limit.

All this continued for many years. I was dissatisfied with my situation, but I didn't know how to institute change. I often felt that I wasn't getting enough air, that I was being squeezed out of the picture by forces I didn't understand. I seemed to be eating for other people, eating foods they liked but I didn't like. For example, if they liked meat and potatoes, I would eat meat and potatoes without giv-

149

ing it a thought. If they said cheese was delicious, I agreed. It had all been crammed down my throat. I hadn't had a minute to find out what I liked. And I was choking on other people's decisions for me. I didn't really like being force-fed.

By the time I tried to do anything about this, I was pretty bent out of shape, as you can imagine. I had no idea what hunger felt like, I had no trust in my own body or mind to help me through a difficult time, I didn't know if I could survive without the program that ran automatically in my head, and I certainly didn't think I was smart enough to know what was good for me. I would do the strangest things: I would have strong reactions to people who meant nothing to me and I would feel that they were denying me sustenance. I would overreact to the presence or absence of supplies. I couldn't take them when someone close to me offered, but I was offended and hurt if they didn't come from emotional strangers. I had no idea how to coax the strangers into giving me anything since I didn't think I should have to do anything to warrant their generosity. The friends, on the other hand, were offering only as a trick to entice me into eating, at which point they would snatch my plate away and call me "greedy."

And so it went until I finally decided that starving and stuffing were wearing me out. Tackling my own hunger seemed like a big job. It required courage. And help. I had been stuffed full of things that might not be useful to me now. I would have to sort out what was life-affirming and what was toxic. I would have to journey into the past to recover my unique story, my individual appetites. I would have to spit out the parts that were hindering my digestion now, and swallow and assimilate what had fed me. I would have to be interested in who I had become, and in the self that had developed and connected with others. I would have to start feeding myself.

Nowadays I know when I've had enough. I can tell the difference between when I've had enough and when I'm still hungry. But even though I've been able to make these distinctions for some time now, I still don't let myself make the next move. The next move would be to act on what I know. When I realize that I've had enough, I can stop doing whatever I'm doing and wait until I want to do it again. I don't have to keep doing it just because it's available at the moment. I could decide that it's not what I want right now. Acting on that knowledge would mean that I am defining my own limits, determining my own boundaries.

I'm not yet willing to set my own limits very often. It seems a terrifying prospect. Being in tune with myself, knowing what my self wants, being able to say yes when I want to, no when I want to, going through my days in my own rhythms, all this seems a dream, a mirage. Because if I could really live my life in my own way, I'd feel a lot less pain than I do now and I'd experience a lot more satisfaction on a regular basis. I'd be in touch with my own power, my power to exert positive control over my own life, to make the next thing happen, to respond to the next opportunity. I would have to acknowledge and take responsibility for the fact that I am not helpless, nor do I have to remain passive.

It would be a revolution of self, an explosion outward, a casting off of the voices in our heads that keep us feeling oppressed and hungry. For on an individual level, we do have choice and control over our lives. We can't control the social structure we're born into, or the historical times, but within the given context of our lives, we do have the power to stop acting out our conditioning as women. We can objectify that conditioning, as so many of us did during the Woman's Movement, and, at another level, as many of us continue to do in our personal psychotherapy, and refuse to participate in the mindless reenactments of gender for which we were raised as daughters. We can begin to see that it is not in our best interest as living beings to feel inferior to the other gender, to deny ourselves pleasure whenever possible, or to always put the needs of others first.

The above is an excerpt from a friend's letter, in which she describes changes she has undergone during the last few years. In her discussion of self-nurturing, she articulates something about the way all of us are trying, in individual ways, to emerge from daughterhood.

There comes a point when we realize that we are not getting enough—that there is some terrible imbalance in which we give out a great deal, at profound cost to ourselves, and get very little back. Some of us realize it first in the area of work, where being one of the "girls" comes as a shocking awakening to the real world after the relative safety, respect, and protection we received or were led to expect in our families. Dad may flirt with us and then hurt our feelings by returning to Mom, but that does not prepare us for the boss who sexually harasses us as a matter of course.

Women feel the stress, even as we dismiss such situations. We are worn out and easily depressed; we get sick a lot. Some of us realize we're not getting enough in our own families, when day after day goes by in which we have nurtured and aided and done for everyone else and wonder if anyone will ever take care of us. The grateful recipients of all this devotion look at us with annoyed distaste if we ask for a little attention in return, or even for a little time off, ready to do without the attention for the rest. In whatever arena we initially recognize our state, we also realize that we have been in a state of acute deprivation for some time, that our resources are running out. We are run down, fragile, susceptible to attack from inside and outside, from mood swings to viruses to traffic accidents.

We realize, moreover, that we are the ones who nurture, the ones who take care of the ill and the infirm. We have to take care of ourselves when we need care. No man is likely to rescue us. or reward our virtue with respect and tender, loving care. That's *our* job. We keep doing it as long as we can, nurturing others even when we are near the breaking point. We keep hoping others will notice, will intervene, will be sorry when we collapse and can't keep everything running smoothly anymore. But others don't read our messages. They persist in not getting it, in staying dense and ignoring our needs. It becomes clear, sooner or later, that we're going to have to supply our own needs to get anything at all.

If we're good and responsible, and feminine, we can't do

much about giving ourselves what we need. We have been taught to consider steady deprivation (of attention, consideration, resources, freedom) our natural lot in life. We must take for ourselves out of the common pot we cook and prepare only as much as we absolutely need, only enough to get by, to make it possible to continue taking care of others. Subsistence living—spiritually, emotionally, materially—is our allotted share. Everything in excess of that should go to others.

When we become aware of the scarcity of our lives, we usually feel doomed rather than angry. It has gone on for as long as we can remember; it has always been that way. But there are times when that sense of cosmic imbalance, of hideous unfairness, bursts into our consciousness. We understand (momentarily) that we really *are* trapped in a world that means us harm —a world not built for us, that considers us inferior and expendable because we are women—that we are the victims of a gender war.

So we are thrown back on ourselves. We either have to accept a life of constant low-grade oppression, in the hopes of warding off acute oppression—a kind of emotional plea bargaining—or find a more efficient way to nurture ourselves. Deciding to give self-care a serious try, we soon discover, though we are expert at taking care of others, we don't really know how to take care of ourselves.

For one thing, we don't know what we need. Need has always been defined by others, has been a property, a characteristic of others. Books and myths and institutions teach us to define others' needs, but we have no idea what our needs are, not to mention which ones are "legitimate." Need is in direct relation to a goal. We need something in order to have or accomplish something else: air to breathe, deodorant to smell acceptable. We have no idea what we want to accomplish, no sense of what criteria to apply. What would be suitable? Is getting a mild headache every time we dust reason enough to say we *need* an aspirin? Or do we *need* to stop dusting? True, everybody *needs* time for themselves, just to be, without responsibility to others or for others, but how much time? Children need attention. When is our need for free time great or real enough to outweigh a child's need? Is it ever? Just before a collapse? Every other week? Why do we need it?

Men are mandated to "make it," whatever that may mean to any individual or group. They need support in order to make it, keep making it, or keep on trying. What are women supposed to do? We have no purpose, no culturally sanctioned goal to help us define and discover our needs. We are supposed to live for others, and subsistence is all we need for that.

If women persist, if we try to discover what our needs might be, try to learn to eat in a way that is neither "unconscious nor compulsive" we take a tremendous step toward autonomy. We are taught to care for ourselves blindly, behind our own backs, like sleepwalkers. Mom often does not sit down at the table with the rest of the family; she stands there serving them, putting bits of rejects and leftovers into her mouth, just to "get rid" of them. She says that she's not really hungry, or that she can't eat because she's too fat already. Mom is so wrapped up in her concern for others that she forgets to take care of herself.

The message of Mom's behavior to her daughters is that women don't take care of themselves: We must care for the men and the children because we need the men, and later the children, to care for us. Taking care of oneself is a sign of selfishness, of coldness, of not caring for anyone but oneself. That's acceptable, even mysteriously attractive in men, but it's definitely not all right for women. We do our best to keep our nurturance habit low.

Women's needs are prescribed for them: romantic love, marriage, children, a home, and most important, people to love and care for, to feel needed. When we discover we need other things as well, we usually find that these other, more basic, and universal needs somehow always conflict directly with romantic love, marriage, children-and-a-home, and feeling needed.

To overcome our stereotyped role, we have to master, to create out of our own experience, to express, to imagine and to dream, to risk ourselves and to know ourselves, to "make it" every bit as much as men do. Romantic love, as prescribed for women, means swooning and holding our breath, waiting to be chosen, and being passive and swept off our feet. Marriage means agreeing to a profoundly unfair contract, trying to work out an intimate, open relationship under circumstances of dependency and inequality. Children-and-a-home means giving up all major risks and projects, all dreams of change and freedom. And feeling needed means forgetting all aspirations to stardom, all attempts at "making it," all dreams of unabashed glory.

So we must learn to make choices, to select the needs we will gratify. We have to make decisions, not just take what we can use from what's easily and immediately available (which is hard enough for us), but also create opportunities to get what we need. Our goal is to select from a wider array, to think of ourselves as we would of a favorite son rather than a good daughter. We have to learn to shop for ourselves carefully and regularly, to be as picky and demanding when it comes to our interests as we are when it comes to our family's. Quantity is not the issue. Many of us shop compulsively, without much pleasure, without much thought to ourselves. What matters is daring to give to ourselves *exactly* what we want, or the closest to it we can honestly get under the circumstances. In short, we have to go out of our way for ourselves and make a loving fuss over meeting our needs.

But when it comes to ourselves, we often have no idea what criteria to employ. We might excel at picking out the right present for friends and family, and think we know exactly what we'd like others to give us, but that doesn't mean we can give it to ourselves without overwhelming anxiety. We often buy articles we know perfectly well we don't really like because what we really want is too expensive (and not on sale), wrong somehow, frivolous. We're supposed to relate to others altruistically, care for them and be concerned whenever they need us, regardless of who they are or how they treat us. Selectiveness of any kind is a sign of conscious choice, of asserting personal preferences, of a lack of genuine femininity. We do select, of course, but we must always furnish ourselves with a rationale for the choice that includes others, or else suffer from guilt.

Creating access, actually going after something we want, going out of our way, even asking others to go out of their way for our benefit, is worse than active selection. It means we are driven. A woman can criticize the government for the uncontrolled use of nuclear power, but it is "extreme" for her to organize a march on the Pentagon that demands its accountability to citizens. Women should respond to danger, but we should not cause things to happen. If we do try to alter events, we are being unfeminine.

Even if we learn how to select, how to insist on getting what we need or what we want, we still don't know how to chew what we've selected. Chewing is an active process; it requires using material, breaking it down into elements we can use, destroying it for our own use, using it up, consciously biting into it, over and over, until it has become grist for our mill. It requires strength, determination, and a will to master. We have been taught to shy away from things, to give up easily, to get discouraged, to depend on help in unfamiliar matters, to assume we will have trouble learning anything that requires logical thought, imagination, or technical precision. We are taught to cope vaguely, semiconsciously, never quite sure of our methods and whether we could repeat the actions. We chew delicately, slowly, each bite almost a matter of trial and error, a lucky hit. The food breaks down almost in spite of us. If we could, we'd just let it sit in our mouths until it melted of its own accord. Open, active energy is unbecoming in feminine women. Ladies still don't eat much in public, and certainly not greedily, lustfully, with their hands, or with gusto or pleasure.

How could we possibly learn to chew properly when we have to be passive, automatically cooperative, and vague, and if any sign of active interest in the world outside the home is almost immediately interpreted as ruthlessness? By this point, when such realizations hit us, we feel angry. We feel cheated and vindicated at the same time, a triumphant kind of anger. There is endless, incredibly clear evidence of the unfairness of it all. Everywhere we look there is further evidence. It was there all the time, but we didn't see it, or we interpreted it in what now seems an incredibly convoluted way just to escape realizing the simple, glaring truth: We are not being treated right. "I *am* being treated badly; it's not my imagination; it's not my fault. They're asking the impossible of me and then blaming me for not delivering!"

That first flash of anger is terribly important for women. Without it, we would give up right at the start, when the scope of the problem, the unfairness, the oppression first become visible to us, when we start to suspect that this is much bigger and much closer than we ever thought. The anger allows us to go further, to face the fact that there is more trouble to be discovered.

Because when we determine to learn how to chew, to actually bite into things openly, and not to mind if it displeases those we love, if we risk their disapproval as well as their displeasure, we discover, by way of reward, that we don't know what to do with the stuff we have chewed up at great cost. The people we love may come around and accept our reality, our public needs and drives. But those others are not the only problem it turns out. There is also the problem within: We don't know how to digest, how to use things for our own good, how to break them down further, past internalization, and integrate them into our system. We don't know how our system works; we don't even know what our system consists of. Our nature has been kept a secret from us. There are prescriptions for being feminine and masculine, but there is very little information, relatively speaking, on what women are really like.

We are told what we should be like, not what we are. We try to comply. We try to stifle the mounting fear that we are totally different from what we're supposed to be, and that we don't know what to do about it. We shut our eyes, grit our teeth, and hold our breath; we try to stop everything in us that is not as it should be, but we just can't do it. We keep screwing up, losing control, giving in. As a result, we can't absorb anything because everything is clamped shut. We can't process our own experiences, can't face new insights, can't pursue novel thoughts. Digestion is an unconscious process. To do it well, we have to let go, to trust our bodies' ways, to listen and attend to those ways and to stop interfering with them. We have to relax, to stop sending unnecessary acid to the rescue, to kill that food, to prevent it from nurturing us too easily. How can we let go and trust our bodies when we know they are inadequate, impure, and imperfect, and when we have no idea how they really work and no real way to find out? (Most doctors won't tell us, and we have not been taught to trust our ability to read and understand scientific material presented in textbooks.)

A woman can get a "sensitive stomach" instead, a properly feminine stomach. It hurts a lot of the time, can't deal with anything rough, acts up totally out of her control, and prevents her from growing up and enjoying herself. Or a woman can gain a great deal of weight, proving that she's not digesting her food, not taking it in and using it on her own behalf. She just stores it in layers of protective fat and uses it as armor against the world. She exists somewhere within, trapped in the armor, invisible to the outside and protected by it. She doesn't integrate the nurturance she takes in; she just uses it to make herself safer in some way.

Women often use whatever nurturance we have managed to wrest from the environment, selecting and openly chewing it at great risk, in a way that does little immediate good. We just have to keep doing it. If we persist, maybe find some way of opening up our internal processes to the light of analysis and comprehension, we may learn to digest. If we get help, begin therapy, join a consciousness-raising group or a support group or a study group that reads books about women, or find friends with whom we can discuss these ideas and perceptions openly, we may be able to let whatever skills we have developed in attending to others take over and take care of us as well. We may learn that survival is not all we can expect. But then we are soon confronted with the next problem: We do not know how to stop eating.

We can initiate the process, create nurturance, select what's good for us, chew and digest it, but we have no idea when and how to stop. We either stop at some early, arbitrary point, after we have consumed a certain magical number of calories, or a certain magical amount of food, or we go on and on, eating until well after we have satisfied our original impulse to eat. We eat until time, food, or opportunity runs out on us. Sometimes we eat to the point of pain. Mostly we eat to obey some command that has nothing much to do with the chemical state of our digestive systems, and whether they could use some new input, and if so, what kind.

We don't eat to satisfy a need, but to suppress a feeling. The problem is that we still can't control why and when we eat, even after we have worked out what we eat and how we eat it. We have learned (in our own interest) a number of mechanisms that enable us to survive, to carry on, to suppress feelings that would get in the way of the carrying on. We let others determine what we do, what we need, what and how much we want. We have no idea how to set limits for ourselves. We are supposed to endure, not to determine. We are supposed to like being controlled from without, being filled with someone else, being tied down by the needs and desires of others. If we call a halt and declare a limit, we are considered rigid and unfeminine. Masochism, on the other hand, may seem weird, but it is certainly not unfeminine. Saints are masochists—mysterious, a little titillating and attractive. Men may shake their heads over us masochists, just as some women do over men who consider any sign of humanity in themselves a basic weakness and lack of masculinity. But then, opposites attract!

We are ready to get angry. We realize we have been robbed of our birthright, the ability to take care of ourselves in basic ways. We are lemmings, doomed by our own inability to change. We are aware that we are caught in a double bind. The vicious cycle goes like this: We have been brought up to take everything without protest, to eat everything on our plates gratefully and cheerfully, to be thankful there is anything on our plates to begin with; at the same time, we have been told to watch out constantly, never to miss an opportunity because there might never be another, and to fear constantly that we might be missing something if we turn away for a second. The demands of femininity have made us passive, ready to endure and swallow anything that parents, husbands, lovers, children, and institutions dish out to us. The nuclear family and its inherent scarcity have forced us to become vigilant and covertly greedy, ready to jump on any scrap that has been carelessly left on the table. It's that or nothing. We need more than we can ever get and are constantly hungry. We are willing to do almost anything to keep the lifeline open and the supplies trickling in, so we are forced to collaborate in our own oppression, to comply with impossible demands and unfair rules—because we can't say no ("Eat that plate clean!") and because it is our only chance at any nourishment at all, as far as we know.

We feel robbed of some of the tools we need to combat the oppressive bind we're caught in. Since we don't know when we're hungry, we don't have the basis on which to make the decision to care for ourselves. We also don't know when we're not hungry anymore, and thus have no way to make decisions for ourselves, no power to set limits, define territories, or insist that the world respect our boundaries. We don't know what our boundaries are. We don't know where others, those who need us, leave off and we begin. We don't know what's our business and what isn't. We're not even sure our bodies belong to us.

If we can't afford enough anger to fuel our journey, or if we've been too suppressed to allow our buried and hidden rage to surface, the glimpse we've had of the sheer magnitude of our predicament is enough to overwhelm us. We become trapped in feeling helpless, in feeling that we are not capable of learning how to nurture ourselves at this late stage with all the odds against us. We interpret further evidence of our oppression as signs of our own ignorance. We decide we're out of control, that we cannot afford to start rectifying the bad situation because we don't know what we're doing and we'd only make things worse, or that we won't know when to stop, or that we'll turn into raving maniacs obsessed with revenge or trapped in a rage that must either remain impotent or become so great and unnatural as to bring the world to a stop. And then we will be responsible for overthrowing the very nature of the world. We are grandiose in our fear of our own rage; we see the world as little, brittle, and in need of care and imagine we could harm it, scar it, or destroy it as we could our helpless children.

We see a struggle of scarcity between mothers and children: Will the children manage to exploit and use up the mother in order to grow before she gives out and is of no further use to them? Or will the mother suppress and reject her children, even at the expense of their full growth, to ensure her own survival?

We see the same kind of struggle between husband and wife: Will his ego needs destroy any chance of her development before she realizes it? Or will she take charge and seek nourishment for herself before he has been properly fed and lose her husband and the support she needs to risk this painful and difficult rebellion against the established order of things?

We feel hopeless, helpless, ignorant, out of control, and frightened. If we allow those feelings to stop us, we stay feminine and agree to continue a life of servitude for the dim hope of rescue and repayment.

If we can free up enough rage from eating ourselves up inside and use it to carry us across this terrible realization of our inferior state, we have to prepare for a period of acute and constant anxiety and deep depression. Eventually the shock of recognition may wear off, but the newly discovered reality remains. We see how bad our position is but don't know what to do about it. We feel undermined and impotent. It takes time to discover how bad things really are, and it means living with impotence. We resist the truth at first, and keep resisting it, even after we have seen and understood enough so that truth should no longer come as surprising news.

We think there might be another explanation, that the old (or new) self-serving explanations invented by men may be right after all. We think this even if we know there is no single truth, that all that matters is having a way to articulate a truth for ourselves that is equally self-serving, but in our service rather than in others'. We feel uncertain even after realizing that what matters is having our own perspective, not assuming that men know best about women. We still resist what we see because it is too discrepant with everything we've been taught, everything we've believed and hoped for, everything we've seen in a different light. It makes us feel unreal, as though we're throwing off a whole skin, a whole mind set, a whole identity without a clear sense that another lies underneath or is in the making. We start to feel too alienated, too different, too weird. It's unsettling to walk around seeing the world differently from everyone around you. We begin to sound different; we're accused of being humorless, preoccupied, of being on a soap box all the time.

We see that the structures we've come to depend on are really arbitrary or crazy or inimical to us. We remember our secure, unconscious state as if it had been a blessed one. We envy women who apparently feel fine about serving their enemies because we were used to eating for other people. We feel anxious, guilty, and clumsy when we eat for ourselves, so we get little joy or satisfaction from our occasional, timid attempts to do so. We didn't really like being force-fed, but sometimes, when we are overwhelmed by the struggle ahead, it seems infinitely preferable to having to go out there—into the kitchen or into the world—and do it for ourselves.

But it no longer seems feasible to continue spending a one and only life being force-fed for someone else's good. Force-feeding is a dreadful contradiction: It involves feeding, an activity meant to satisfy our needs and help us to live and grow and develop. At the same time, it involves force, invasion, and outside control.

In addition to constant anxiety, alienation, feeling unreal, out of touch, and endangered, we also experience a crushing depression. The magnitude of the discovery alone is enough to depress us. It means, at that point, that there is no hope. Depression, psychotherapists tell us, is a result of severe loss or repressed anger. We're facing both. The loss is the hope itself: the promise that kept us going, the symbolic and largely unconscious covenant we thought we could rely on. Now we have to relinquish all illusion of health, happiness, of virtue's just reward.

If the world is designed to keep women down, and if the design has been the blueprint for the institutions that have shaped and controlled our lives for many centuries, possibly for all of recorded history, what can we hope for? So we lose hope and discover that we must also lose any help we might find in our environment. Our rage, the very energy that has brought us to this point, alienates others. We end up getting less than ever from them because we're no longer playing by the rules. How can we expect men to give up their age-old privileges for us at the same moment we find everything they do selfish, rigid, tyrannical, soulless, and ruthless? What's in it for them? They either hang in there, hurt and angry themselves but willing to wait until we come to our "senses" or leave us to find a woman still willing to play by the old rules. (Some men who reject and abandon us because we're trying to emancipate ourselves are perfectly capable of appreciating a "liberated woman" who is sexy, feisty, and independent, as long as she doesn't give them a hard time. They even benefit from her freedom to enjoy herself more, to be more interesting, more self-involved, more dynamic, and more glamorous.)

But if we try to suppress our anger, if we sit on it and try to make the best of our lot, try to contain our knowledge in one compartment of our minds, try to carry on as before and smooth things over, we're no better off. Expressing our anger leads to loss in the short run, and suppressing it leads to another kind of loss: a loss of the very self we have just started to consider, if only intellectually. It's like discovering that something real survived underneath the feminine coating, and then having to give it up or put it back into the deep freeze.

The contradictions of femininity have surfaced. We see them and feel anxious and depressed. If we persist again, if we go on examining the evidence, if we trust ourselves to sit with the anxiety that accompanies going through these changes, if we allow the dust to settle, we can eventually distinguish the bleak landscape of oppression before us from specific obstacles to change in our lives. If we are willing to climb the first mountain—it's true that it's only one and there are countless others—we learn that we can climb. We begin to appreciate the difficulty and significance of our struggles, the importance of coming to terms with our own situation in the world.

If we are lucky, we find an environment in which to express, nurture, and reward those feelings, a community or a group of women undergoing similar revelations. If these are hard to come by, we must nurture these feelings ourselves, allow and plan for and try to facilitate them in ourselves. We must create occasions that allow us to be inspired by our own potential courage, essential beauty, and worth. We must appeal to ourselves, fantasize ourselves the heroines, once again, of our own stories. Many of us must nurture the growing, conscious part of ourselves in private or in secret for a long time before it is strong enough to withstand daylight.

In the protective community of women, we can afford to examine the fantasy as well as the reality. We must come to recognize, in a place where no one blames us, that the obstacles are internal as well as external. We must be validated in our perception of the world and supported in our exploration of our own internal economy. In this environment, it is given that whatever our internal state of affairs turns out to be, it's all right, it's fine, it's welcome. We need a chance to sort out what in us is authentic from what is programmed for exploitation and victimization. We have to get to know who we are. We have to learn to recognize when our own apparently spontaneous responses are appropriate to our own interests and when they are overreactions; in the latter case we have to learn what triggers those reactions and why. We become interested in such explorations because we have come to realize that a large part of our "spontaneous" response to situations is actually preprogrammed in ways that don't really serve us but force us to accept a great deal of frustration. We become disconcertingly self-conscious because we can't do much to intervene on our own behalf. We have no idea of our identity without that program; that other part of us is just a child who can't be expected to negotiate the world because she doesn't know how. She needs a safe place to grow up in before she can *do* anything!

So we regress, fall back on old ways that never helped much anyway but that caused predictable outcomes: fights, rejections —it doesn't matter as long as it's familiar. We often find ourselves back in the old family romance and realize that we went out of our way to fall into the trap, that we may even have been full partners in creating it. We have several options: We can blame ourselves, blame someone else, or suspend blame and keep looking at it. If we blame ourselves, if we call ourselves pathological for valiant attempts to adapt to an untenable situation, we avoid the sadness, grief, and disappointment we prefer to deny. If we blame others, we may be more in touch with our disappointment and loss, but we keep alive the fantasy that others are responsible for the course of our lives and our present status. Thus we can continue to hope that we will someday be rescued (usually by men who will love and understand us as our present partners cannot). Meanwhile we continue to feel isolated, bitter, and hopeless and do nothing to address our own problems. Our other alternative is to suspend blame, to recognize it as a perfectly understandable desire, but not necessarily act upon it.

We want to blame others to make the disaster accessible to our control. We point the finger and accuse others, hoping that if they are the cause, they are also the solution. Blaming someone else is not a step toward a solution unless it is followed up with serious attempts at change, and it is a blind alley unless it is based on a thorough analysis of the situation. Blaming others is useless if we are not willing to go further and examine our own feelings when we want to place blame elsewhere for our situation. Other people are as equally unable to stop being who they were forced to become as we are.

Then there is the situation itself, our position in relation to men—our femininity in contrast to their masculinity. We may see evidence of inequality all over the place, but we have to get to the point of trying to figure out, seriously and systematically, whatever our systems of analysis, what the evidence means. We have to ask ourselves why we think we are and have been historically oppressed, and what we can and wish to do to combat the causes of our oppression. It goes without saying that we have to ask ourselves how we intend to deal with the symptoms of the oppression, both in ourselves and in others.

We have to analyze our situation further to find a way to formulate criteria for ourselves that will help us select what we will work on. The magnitude of the task makes us feel little and helpless, so we have to break it down into digestible particles. Finding a framework for ourselves—art, biology, social history, economics, psychology—is a way to start the process of digestion. It is a method for insisting on mastery, for declaring that we consider ourselves equal to the problem—because we are worth a try at success. However we do it, we are declaring war on the prevailing conditions, stepping out of role, acting in an unfeminine manner, showing a serious interest in ourselves.

We have to discover what, of all the things we were stuffed with, is "life affirming" and what is "toxic." We have to learn to stop poisoning and to start feeding ourselves. To do that we have to understand how events affect us, what we want, like, are good at, afraid of, angry about. Most of us are not sure of any of that, it's all so confused with myth and art and accidents of history. And it is extremely difficult to maintain the kind of perspective—an almost "objective" interest in ourselves, without blame—that we need to help us discover who we are or could be if we weren't stuck in the rules of gender.

This analysis can be exhilarating, a great high, but it can also be painful and depressing. Only structure helps us through. That's where our good-girl training might be used to our advantage: If we can get compulsive and reliable about taking care of ourselves, there may be no stopping us!

But we need permission. It is too frightening. We have been programmed to avoid this very kind of self-consciousness. Too much in us—defenses that helped us through the minefield of childhood and that it would be suicidal to give up now without a fight—mitigates against our staying focused on ourselves with benign interest. We need help, perhaps from a group of like-minded friends or a therapist. We need someone who will find whoever we turn out to be intrinsically O.K., in an environment where we don't have the usual things to lose. Permission to stay in touch with ourselves, to see what we see and digest it, has to come from that outer source, at least to some extent. Somebody has to honestly agree with us and validate our perceptions. Everyone needs that. We have been taught, however, to seek that impartial benign friend in those closest to us, by definition an impossible task. We may get a lot of support from some of our families or partners, but starting with and depending on them for aid leads up a blind alley. We must get outside help in whatever form. In many ways, the first step in emerging from daughterhood, the first major act of self-nourishing, involves getting ourselves to a place of potential support and then asking for it.

Asking is an act of great courage. We are quite well equipped to deny and repress whatever momentary sense of an authentic, unlimited self we may have experienced by seeking support. Just another strong, romantic feeling, another fantasy. We can use the experience to hone our cynicism or put ourselves down. But if we find our way through that labyrinth and ask for support, we have already risked a great deal and won. We can only nourish ourselves adequately if we acknowledge our need and feed ourselves when we are hungry.

The implications of what we have bitten off and started to chew surface slowly. They become clear as we start to act on what we know. First, we have to decide to act. Because the need for change seems so vast and overwhelming, our real task is to delineate a problem, something in relation to which we can take a first step. Opportunities for acting "differently" exist all the time. We have to understand what we are doing, what's at stake, and what could result from giving up the old program in our heads. Though it is not the only thing, what's at stake in almost all cases is *gender loss*.

As far back as we can remember, the dimensions along which people have been granted honor or chosen for leadership seem bound up with age and gender. Age is the flexible dimension: As it changes and we get older it reinforces us in the hope that someday we will really be grown-ups with all the power we always thought grown-ups had. Gender is the immutable dimension. Gender determines, or is said to determine, practically every aspect of our behavior. We are supposed to do things differently, feel differently, and think differently, depending on gender. The script for each gender is complex but clear enough. We learn it early and keep on learning it. It determines who we are. It is the most powerful, and apparently comprehensible, guideline we have. We are either good girls or bad ones, princesses or witches. There is no question of becoming princes or pirates or even presidents. Yet we always realize that our own, personal hold on the laws of gender, so apparently ancient and immutable, is relatively shaky. We don't always act in feminine ways, but more important, we often have profound and powerful impulses in the opposite direction. We want to act like men. Sometimes we do act like men. Sometimes we take over and brag and master and shout and deal and produce and insist. When we start feeling like men, when the sin catches up with us, we feel gross—clumsy, ugly, ungainly, unlovable, and pathetic and disappointing. We know that our moms and dads would not be happy if they saw us now. We feel like impostors and frauds and perverts, or just funny and uncomfortable or embarrassed enough never to try that trick again!

Whatever its form, we experience gender loss and are terrified. Gender was the only meaningful guideline given us; we don't know that we can give it up. We can't know that not acting like a woman is not synonymous with acting like or becoming a man. We have no way of knowing that if we cease to act like victims we won't turn into victimizers.

There are only two genders, as far as we've been told, and they are absolute and immutable. If one is born female, she must act feminine or be considered and treated as a human failure. The same goes for a male who does not act masculine. If one is born female and acts masculine, she is not accepted into the world of men but is considered a pervert, a lunatic, or a criminal menace. Gender loss involves a terrifying sense of loss of identity, of stepping on forbidden ground, of breaking taboos and waiting for the gods to strike us dead or dumb. One part of that breathless feeling of having the rug pulled out from under us is excitement: The gender bounds have been loosened, things could possibly change. If the rules are not unbreakable, then maybe there are no rules!

The excitement is important and must be nourished. It gets us to the next step. We must also recognize, accept, and deal with anxiety. Some anxiety makes sense: If we pursue the path toward autonomy, we will run up against opposition, ridicule, hatred, and contempt in some form. We have every reason to be cautious and wary. But parts of anxiety are not rational; they are rooted within us, myths we have internalized and that have become the stories we tell ourselves to explain our situation: We're stupid, worthless, lazy, bad, incompetent, failures.

But what if all our premises got turned upside down? What if the unshakable notion that sexual feelings appear only in relation to men were to be undermined? What if we wish to consummate the intense, helpful, exciting, rewarding complex, even neurotic relationships we have with women? What if we fall in love with women? Or what if we just lust after women? What if we want to be cared for by women the way men have been? What if we want to be selfish and greedy and tyrannical and proud and ruthless too? What if everything we learned the hard way about being women turns out to be useless? What if we really have no idea whatsoever who we are and what makes us tick, and we don't know much more about anyone else? What if we never wanted to be mothers or wives? What will happen to us? Will we burst out of our feminine straitjackets as the Incredible Hulk does when he bursts out of the clothes of mild-mannered David Banner? Will we say or do something unforgivable and end up, our bridges irretrievably burned, across the river with no place to go, helpless and hopeless again?

Gender loss threatens the foundations, or what we have been taught to consider the foundations of our very selves. It is not, however, an objective danger: We will not turn into men by acting autonomously. We will merely appear to some to be acting unseemly; to others we will be a source of support in the struggle to break with gender prescriptions. We will, however, risk losing our sense of gender, our sense of what is given and must never be questioned, and what is questionable and must be thought about. Very little remains if we question gender. We must think about everything and decide anew. That leaves plenty of space for error, misinformation, misunderstanding, and just plain thoughtlessness. We are apt to make things a lot harder on ourselves than we absolutely need to when we first decide to risk gender loss. Later, we may become better at it, less likely to draw fire.

We are in a very vulnerable position. Gender is a mental construct laid upon our physiology arbitrarily and with intent. It is an arbitrary distinction among humans used to enslave at least half the population. There are racial and other distinctions, including class and age, that subdivide again and determine the hierarchy within the dominant gender, on an equally arbitrary basis. This is not to say that differences do not exist, but only that they in no way prescribe the rules laid down on each group. Nothing much follows from the fact that we have a female reproductive system, or what does follow is unclear and not related to the rules we live by.

But gender is a concept that has been used to explain practically everything we wanted to know as we learned to negotiate the world. It has become a powerful, magical incantation, a taboo we know is not safe to ignore. We have heard what can happen to people: There is real persecution and real punishment for offenders against the gender laws. Lesbians are not considered real women. A lesbian, who lives her life relating to women, caring for women, loving women, fighting and feuding with women, is routinely told that she wouldn't act that way if she was "normal." She is being unfeminine by being interested in herself and her own kind. She is told, by the psychiatric establishment, for instance, that she is immature and arrested in her development. She is told that she should love people who are unlike herself and accept the fact that all women are incomplete without the other gender, that women and men, but especially women, are nothing without each other.

A heterosexual woman, who loves men as well as she can, is told that she is immature in not being satisfied with her apparent inequality inside the relationship, that she tries to castrate men out of penis envy, that she must accept men as they are and change herself to please men, that therein lies women's fulfillment and reward. And a woman who involves herself with a man who is not very masculine, who likes to play it different ways, who is concerned with analogous questions about his own gender, is called domineering and is pitied, because a "real" woman needs a man who dominates her. She would be much less strident, much happier, if only she had the right macho man to put her in her place.

Such attitudes may seem ridiculous, well exposed, outdated to some, but they are the prevailing norm, and they are not about to wither away under the sheer power of our analysis. We women have to find a way to live our lives and support each other in the struggle under the present circumstances.

Support from women, from others who are asking themselves similar questions, who are determined to emerge from deforming daughterhoods, is necessary to every woman. Recognizing gender as only a construct, that nothing follows from it, that it is not the way the world need always be divided, is very radical. It undermines the basic tenets of much of what we know as our civilization. Keeping such a vision, however cloudy, to ourselves is like being enveloped in a kind of madness. We need to touch someone else with a similar vision to know we are not crazy.

Like the friend whose letter appeared at the beginning of this chapter, we often know what the problem is, but don't know what to do with that knowledge, don't know how to act on it. Other women can help. If nothing else, they can help us recognize what steps we have already taken and are continuing to take. We don't always give ourselves credit for what we have already done. We have risked rejection and gender loss over and over; we have survived it and made our peace with it to some extent. We have found innumerable imaginative solutions to problems that way, but we all have lines we are afraid to overstep and fears we will go too far. Holding someone's hand while stepping over a line together can make it possible. Realizing by discussion, sharing, consciousness-raising, therapy, that we know how to do what we have to do also can make it possible. What we need, to escape the prison of our feminine training, is to recognize that we get what we need only in spite of our faithful adherence to femininity, not because of it. The Princess in us may get some of what we need and some of what we want, but the price is unnecessarily high and the return ridiculously low and unreliable. The Good Girl in us may still hope for her reward at the end of the long walk into the sunset, but she has to accept deprivation until then and realize her hope is fanciful and hardly ever fulfilled.

We have to take ourselves in hand and risk our peace of mind, our comfort and safety. We must recognize that the contradictions of femininity are strangling all of us, that we have to help ourselves in the struggle for autonomy and self-determination. We must take over and use the program in a new way, risk mistakes and losses and difficult times. We are on a journey that is hard and long. We must trust ourselves to go the distance.

BIBLIOGRAPHY

Allen, Charlotte Vale. *Daddy's Girl*. New York: Wyndham Books, 1980.

Arcana, Judith. *Our Mothers' Daughters*. Berkeley: Shameless Hussy Press, 1979.

Armstrong, Louise. *Kiss Daddy Goodnight*. New York: Hawthorn Books, 1978.

Bowlby, John. *Attachment and Loss*. Vol. 1, *Attachment*. New York: Basic Books, 1969.

————. *Attachment and Loss*. Vol. 2, *Separation—Anxiety and Anger*. New York: Basic Books, 1973.

Brady, Katherine. *Father's Days*. New York: Seaview Books, 1979.

Brownmiller, Susan. *Against Our Will: Men, Women and Rape*. New York: Simon and Schuster, 1975.

Carter, Angela. *The Sadeian Woman*. New York: Pantheon Books, 1978.

Chodorow, Nancy. *The Reproduction of Mothering: Psychoanalysis and the Sociology of Gender*. Berkeley: University of California Press, 1978.

de Beauvoir, Simone. *The Second Sex*. New York: Alfred A. Knopf, 1953.

Dinnerstein, Dorothy. *The Mermaid and the Minotaur*. New York: Harper and Row, 1976.

Douglas, Mary, ed. *Rules and Meanings: The Anthropology of Everyday Knowledge*. New York: Penguin Books, 1973.

Flax, Jane. "The Conflict Between Nurturance and Autonomy in Mother-Daughter Relationships and Within Feminism," *Feminist Studies* 4, no. 2 (June 1978): 71–91.

Freud, Sigmund. *Standard Edition of Complete Psychological Works of Sigmund Freud*, ed. James Strachey. London: Hogarth Press, 1957–1964.

Friday, Nancy. *My Mother/My Self*. New York: Delacorte Press, 1977.

Gilbert, Lucy, and Paula Webster. "Femininity: The Sickness Unto Death." Paper presented at The Second Sex—Thirty Years Later:

A Commemorative Conference on Feminist Theory. New York University, 1979.

Goffman, Erving. *Gender Advertisements*. New York: Harper Colophon Books, 1979.

———. *Interaction Ritual*. New York: Anchor Books, 1967.

Hammer, Signe. *Daughters and Mothers: Mothers and Daughters*. New York: Quadrangle, New York Times Book Co., 1975.

Haskell, Molly. *From Reverence to Rape: The Treatment of Women in the Movies*. New York: Holt, Rinehart and Winston, 1974.

Herman, Judith Lewis. *Father-Daughter Incest*. Cambridge: Harvard University Press, 1981.

Horney, Karen. *Feminine Psychology*. New York: W. W. Norton, 1967.

Kohut, Heinz. *The Analysis of the Self*. New York: International Universities Press, 1971.

Lerner, Harriet. "Internal Prohibitions Against Female Anger." *American Journal of Psychoanalysis*, vol. 40, no. 2 (1980): 137–147.

Mahler, Margaret. *On Human Symbiosis and the Vicissitudes of Individuation*. Vol. 1, *Infantile Psychosis*. New York: International Universities Press, 1968.

———. *The Psychological Development of the Human Infant*. New York: Basic Books, 1976.

Memmi, Albert. *The Colonizer and the Colonized*. Boston: Beacon Press, 1967.

Miller, Alice. *Prisoners of Childhood*. New York: Basic Books, 1981.

Miller, Jean Baker. *Toward a New Psychology of Women*. Boston: Beacon Press, 1976.

Millett, Kate. *The Basement: Meditations on a Human Sacrifice*. New York: Simon and Schuster, 1979.

Mitchell, Juliet. *Psychoanalysis and Feminism*. New York: Pantheon Books, 1974.

Orbach, Susie. *Fat Is a Feminist Issue*. New York: Paddington Press, 1978.

Pizzey, Erin. *Scream Quietly or the Neighbours Will Hear*. Harmondsworth, England: Penguin Books, 1974.

Rich, Adrienne. *Of Woman Born: Motherhood as Experience and Institution*. New York: W. W. Norton, 1976.

Rubin, Gayle. "The Traffic in Women: Notes on the 'Political Economy' of Sex," in R. Reiter, ed., *Towards an Anthropology of Women.* New York: Monthly Review Press, 1975.

Russell, Diana. *The Politics of Rape: The Victim's Perspective.* New York: Stein and Day, 1975.

Slater, Philip. *Earthwalk.* New York: Anchor Books/Doubleday, 1974.

Walker, Lenore. *The Battered Woman.* New York: Harper Colophon Books, 1979.

Webster, Paula. "The Politics of Rape in Primitive Society," *Heresies: A Feminist Publication on Art and Politics,* vol. 6 (1978).

Winnicott, D. W. *The Maturational Processes and the Facilitating Environment.* New York: International Universities Press, 1965.

———. *Playing and Reality.* New York: Basic Books, 1971.

Lucy Gilbert is a psychotherapist in private practice in New York City, specializing in work with women who have experienced violence in their lives. She received her Ph.D. in developmental psychology from Columbia University.

Paula Webster is codirector of the Institute for the Study of Sex in Society and History, New York City. She is presently working on a book about sexual repression, and holds a master's degree in anthropology from the University of Michigan.